"WOW...Pastor Ellen Laitinen s book is a journey that takes us through the tremendous insights and experiences that have led her to write this very inspiring book on Prophetic Intercession. *ADVANCING KINGDOM PURPOSES THROUGH PROPHETIC INTERCESSION* helps to clear up many misunderstandings between intercessors and leadership of the Church. It takes people from a simple hunger for prayer across a rich and mature bridge of how God advances His kingdom through prayer. I am so pleased with this book and would love to recommend it to every person with a heart to pray, every pastor that cares that their people understand the benefit of prophetic intercession, and for all those who desire to experience a greater effectiveness in ministry.

In this book, Pastor Ellen helps us to sort out the many issues in dealing with prophetic prayer as well as provides a clear understanding of how to bring a prayer ministry into a whole new level of function within the body of Christ world-wide. You should not miss the revelation nor the heart of Pastor Ellen to capture you for a while in reading this book. *ADVANCING KINGDOM PURPOSES THROUGH PROPHETIC INTERCESSION* will impact your life and assist you with your ministries. I promise you will never be the same!"

--Bishop Richard Callahan
Proceeding Word Ministries
Orlando, Florida

"Anything that can be done without prayer is not really worth doing.

Jesus said, "without me you can do nothing", but he also said "we are not without Him", so 'with Him' we can do the impossible.

"Wow!" Pastor Ellen has written a powerful and very thorough book on prophetic intercession. Previously, the subject of prophetic intercession had been sadly neglected in Christian literature.

God gave "all power" to Jesus and Jesus bestowed "all power' unto the church. Now, it is up to you and I to wield this Kingdom power and Kingdom authority to bind and loose on Earth what Jesus has already bound in Heaven.

Pastor Ellen urges us with God's mandate to prophetically intercede for the lost world, for the sick anemic church, and for those who are demon oppressed and sick. God invites us to enter into Biblical prophetic intercession, and if we do, we will bring His Kingdom and glory to people everywhere.

In this book, you will discover "the ways and the hows" to successfully wage spiritual warfare with the "war weapons" of intercession, discernment, gifts of the Spirit, wisdom and knowledge. This is God's answer to the present world crisis. Now is the time – Now go do it.

Thank you Pastor Ellen for this most needed and vital book."

--Apostle Emanuele Cannistraci
Founder of Apostolic Missions International

"Ellen Laitinen has discovered one of the most powerful secrets of effective prayer. She knows that prayer is not just about us asking God for what we want, but about us praying what the Holy Spirit wants! This is true prophetic intercession-- allowing God to lead, guide and speak clearly as we pray according to His plan. I am so thankful that someone has written such a practical resource for intercessors and ministry leaders. It is a vital tool for every local church."

--Lee Grady
Contributing Editor, Charisma Magazine
Director, The Mordecai Project

"The Body of Christ needs this book! To be honest, prophetic intercessors have often made me very nervous. I've seen churches split as a result of intercessory prayer teams in conflict with church leaders - how ironic! But, if churches embrace the insightful and practical truths Ellen shares in this book, they will experience both unity in their churches and supernatural power in their ministries! This book should be required reading for every pastoral staff and prayer team!"

--Jim Johnson
Berlin, Germany
Missionary/Church Planter
Author, *Transforming Grace: God's Path to Inward Change*

The role of the "prophetic intercessor" in a local congregation is vital to the overall spiritual health of a church. The intercessor's devotion to Christ and his or her unswerving commitment to the leadership, vision, and goals of the church, is a strength every pastor should have in place, undergirding all of the church's ministries. Historically, the role of the intercessor has been like the story of Cinderella. We, in church leadership, appreciated the work they were doing for us, but kept them in the basement in an attempt to remove them from the more "polished" members of the congregation. However, over the past decade, it is as if they have been discovered and elevated to a prominent position in the Lord's kingdom. Their value to the church has always been great, but they have recently been elevated to an even greater position of honor and significance in many congregations across the world. For anyone who has been caught up in the struggle between pastoral leadership and the men and women gifted in prophetic intercession, Ellen Laitinen's book on *Advancing Kingdom Purposes Through Prophetic Intercession* will be an enriching experience. She goes way beyond theoretical insights into the practical application of establishing and maintaining a dynamic prayer ministry in a local church. I especially appreciate the way she handles the relationship between the pastor and the prophetic intercessor. Her wisdom concerning protocol for these relationships is deeply spiritual and practically applicable. A much needed book for the Body of Christ.

--John Isaacs

Senior Pastor,

Kingsway Community Church, San Jose, CA

"Ellen Laitinen is a seasoned servant of God who has done the Body of Christ a great service with her great insights in the area of prophetic intercession! In recent decades there has been a noticeable divide between many called to intercession and those flowing in the apostolic. As a powerful intercessor under proper apostolic alignment, Ellen's important work, *ADVANCING KINGDOM PURPOSES THROUGH PROPHETIC INTERCESSION*, can help bridge that gap and bring much needed biblical order"

--Dr. Joseph Mattera
Senior Pastor of Resurrection Church
Presiding Bishop of Christ Covenant Coalition
Author, *Kingdom Revolution*

"This much needed book explains the often misunderstood art of prophetic prayer in an in-depth, well balanced and wise fashion with an emphasis on blessing local churches and partnering with pastors. A must handbook for intercessors and those who love to pray!"

--Mary-Alice Isleib
Mary Alice Ministries/Christian Outreach International

Advancing Kingdom Purposes
Through
Prophetic Intercession

Sandie -
May the Lord
illuminate the eyes
of your understanding,
to know the hope of
your calling with an increased
fullness! Many blessings.
Pastor SW
Eph 3:20

Advancing Kingdom Purposes Through Prophetic Intercession

ISBN: 1449916406
EAN-13: 9781449916404

Scripture Quotations:

Any bold highlighting, italics or underlining of Scriptures, are emphasis added by the author of this book.

All Scripture quotations, unless otherwise indicated, are taken from the New King James Version. Copyright © 1982 by Thomas Nelson, Inc. Used by permission. All rights reserved.

Scripture quotations marked (NIV) are taken from the HOLY BIBLE, NEW INTERNATIONAL VERSION®. NIV®. Copyright © 1973, 1978, 1984 by International Bible Society. Used by permission of Zondervan. All rights reserved.

Scripture quotations marked (NLT) are taken from the Holy Bible, New Living Translation, Copyright © 1996. Used by permission of Tyndale House Publishers, Inc., Wheaton, Illinois 60189. All rights reserved.

Cover Design:
Shaun Middlebusher
Graphics Director
Rhema Graphix Solutions
shaun@rhemagraphix.com
www.rhemagraphix.com

Contents

v

Foreword

Prayer is a major passion in my life. It's been that way since I was first saved as a hungry teenager. Our church back then was small, but it was truly a house of prayer. My wife and I met at one of our all-night prayer meetings! Today, I serve as the Senior Pastor of that same church. As our work around the world has grown, our commitment to prayer has increased all the more. Whether praying in our church, our city or on divine assignments in cities and nations around the world, I've never forgotten the importance of seeing the Kingdom of God advanced through prayer.

That is why I am excited about the book you now hold in your hands. Intercession is great ministry mosaic composed of a vast array of flows, moods and functions. One of the least understood prayer flows is that of prophetic intercession. In *Advancing Kingdom Purposes Through Prophetic Intercession,* we now have a strong source of teaching and wisdom to extend the church's reach in this vital area.

For the last decade, Ellen Laitinen has partnered with me in the pursuit of God's purposes through prayer. She is not only a graduate of our IMPACT! School of Ministry and an ordained pastor in our church, but she is a wise teacher and sensitive prophetess. She is not just smart. Ellen is caring and experienced. I trust her and respect her. She is a gift to Kathy and me, our ministry team and our entire congregation. Now with this book, she will become a gift to you.

I recommend *Advancing Kingdom Purposes Through Prophetic Intercession* for a number of reasons. First, *this is a unique book.* I am not aware of another one like it. It not only chronicles Ellen's personal progress as a student of the Spirit, but more importantly, it brings light to a largely unseen and unappreciated expression of intercession. Second, *this is a practical book.* There is no fluff here. If you've been looking for clarity in the area of prophetic intercession, you've found it. Read on, and you will soon see what I mean. Third, *this is a timely book*. As the world struggles to find solutions to the great problems of our day, we need the key of an increased awareness of the prophetic flow in the church. God is calling and empowering a glorious company of men, women and young people to pray His purposes into the earth. Now is the time for a resource like this.

All of this makes me confident that you'll be profoundly grateful for this book. I encourage you to read Ellen's words, search the Scripture, and seek the Lord for your greatest calling in life: to see the Kingdom of God forcefully advance until this whole world has been shaken by His glorious power and unfathomable love.

For His Glory,

David Cannistraci
Senior Pastor
GateWay City Church
San Jose, California
www.davidcannistraci.org

Acknowledgements

With a heart full of gratitude, I wish to express a heartfelt thanks to the following people, many of whom committed to regular weekly fasting and prayer as I wrote. Thank you so much for your words of encouragement and your dedication in praying me through the writing process. So many times I felt like I was riding upon your prayers as I wrote. May your reward return a hundred fold for the tremendous blessing you have been to me.

Karina Arneson

Maryellen Basanese

Joanne Bedekovich

Karen Braxton

Lori Goodrich

Miriam Idle

Jan Keeney

Kate Laitinen

Dad & Sharon Laitinen

Deborah McCoy

Ross & Sandee Miller

Geri Nave

Dory & Jenny Pieters

Nicki Young

And ALL the GateWay intercessors as well as those who have faithfully served on my personal prayer shield who have interceded for me and the vision of this book over the past five years. This has truly been a work in progress and I could not have done it without you!

A BIG thank you to two precious brothers in the Lord, Jonathan Benelli and John McClements, who were willing to assist me in the writing process by sacrificing many hours to serve as my editors. Your expertise in the editing process was truly God-inspired. Thank you to Pastor Jim Johnson, Maryellen Basanese, and Lori Goodrich who took time to meticulously read through this manuscript. Your insights, suggestions, and encouragement were tremendously helpful in the final stages of this manuscript. Thank you to Pastor Gary Avila for your words of encouragement along the way.

A very special thank you to Pastor David Cannistraci who encouraged and mentored me through this writing process by spending countless hours reading through each chapter while in airports, on airplanes, on vacation, and giving me the necessary feedback to refine my thoughts in completing this book.

Over the past 32 years I have been blessed with two very special friends, John and Maryellen Basanese. Initially my youth group counselors and now life-long friends. I will always be grateful for your time and patience with me as a young teenager to share the gospel message and then disciple and challenge me in those foundational truths. Thank you for being His willing vessels to shape my spiritual walk and impart a passion for the deeper things of God. As I complete this book, I am reminded of how much God has used our friendship to transform my life.

And finally, I will always remain eternally grateful for my mother, Sandra Ellen Laitinen, who although she has gone on to be with the Lord, was the one who inspired and imparted a heart for prayer when I was very young.

Dedication

To the men and women over the years who have been part of the Prophetic Intercession Team at GateWay City Church. This book was initially written with you in mind! You were my inspiration in writing down what I hoped would be the foundational principles in understanding prophetic intercession.

May the Lord cause you to rise up into the fullness of all God has destined for you to become. I believe with all my heart that the Lord has personally hand-picked you to serve on this team and caused me to grow as a leader because of you. What a blessing you have been and continue to be! No leader could be more proud of how I have seen each of you allow the Lord to work in and through your lives. I consider each of you to be a precious treasure in my life with your diverse gifts and expressions. Thank you for your faithfulness in standing with me as we continue to stand watch in prayer over how God desires to fulfill His promises and advance His kingdom through our church.

I love each of you so dearly!
and
To two very special senior pastors:
Dr. David Cannistraci
and
Bishop Richard Callahan
I am deeply grateful for all that you have sown into my life and to have had pastors that walk in the kind of integrity that I can follow after.

Introduction

In 1990, as I was preparing for a summer mission trip to Argentina, a prophet declared over my life: "God is giving you three spiritual gifts: the word of wisdom, the word of knowledge, and the discernment of spirits." The activation of these three gifts opened up a whole new dimension of prayer. This was the beginning of a spiritual journey; the Lord was getting ready to use me in brand new ways.

As I share my journey, I want you to have a deeper understanding of prophetic intercession and how it can benefit the local and regional church. I believe that prophetic intercession is essential to the advancement of what God desires to accomplish in the earth today. I do not claim to have all the answers, but my hope is to bring some clarity to this area of prayer as well as to dispel some of the common misperceptions that hinder pastors and prophetic intercessors from co-laboring.

Please note that *intercessors* and *prayer warriors* are terms that will be used interchangeably. They are defined as those with a God-inspired burden to pray. However, it would be a mistake to lump all intercessors into the same category. Even though all intercessors hear from God, not all intercessors are prophetic in the way they pray. This is the great divide: prophetic intercessors versus other prayer warriors, or what I will term general intercessors. Although the central focus for this book will be on prophetic intercession, I will briefly discuss the differences between these two types and how each expression fulfills a necessary role in the body of Christ.

The terms *prophetic intercessor* and *watchman* will also be used interchangeably, since both of these intercessory roles function very similarly. My intention is not to ignore general intercessors, but to bring greater understanding to a realm of intercessory prayer that is not well-understood in the local church. That is not to say that the principles and key concepts shared here are not applicable to other areas of prayer. It is just that my primary focus will be on the prophetic aspect of intercession and how this can further kingdom advancement in the earth.

Advancing Kingdom Purposes
Overview

"The effective and fervent prayer of a righteous man avails much."   *James 5:15b*

Advancing Kingdom Purposes Through Prophetic Intercession is designed to connect two points: **prophetic intercession** and **effective ministry**. One of the critical elements in this advance is the synergy created when pastors and prophetic intercessors are properly connected and in alignment with God's divine purposes. In order to illustrate the importance of this relationship, we need to understand prophetic intercession. The following is an overview of the topics covered.

Defining Prophetic Intercession

What is prophetic intercession and how do we identify who is a prophetic intercessor? In the chapters ahead, we will clarify what prophetic intercession is and where this intercessory expression can be of value in the body of Christ. We will explore the indicators of believers called to this type of prayer and the four spiritual gifts that relate to it. You will notice the terms *prophetic gifts* and *revelation gifts* are used interchangeably in reference to these four spiritual gifts. The vantage point from which I write is to offer insight as someone who functions in all four of the prophetic gifts: the Word of Wisdom[1], the Word of knowledge[2], the Discernment of Spirits[3],

---

[1] A sudden knowing of what to do or how to pray.

and Prophecy[4]. Most of how I "perceive" prophetically is an expression of the discernment of spirits. We will discuss the main function for each revelation gift as well as the various types of prophetic manifestations that flow from these four spiritual gifts. In addition, I will highlight some of the key differences between someone who operates in the prophetic through the gift of the discernment of spirits versus the gift of prophecy.

The Prophetic Prayer Flow

One of the distinct differences of an intercessor who is prophetic has to do with how they are focused in prayer. Prophetic intercessors enter into prayer very differently from other prayer warriors because of the revelation they receive as part of their unique expression. Part of this difference involves a tendency to remain focused on the same prayer point for a longer period of time than other prayer warriors. As they go before the Lord in prayer, these intercessors are listening to discern the mind of the Lord in guiding them in how to pray. There are several helpful guidelines that we will review in activating and maintaining this kind of a prophetic prayer flow when praying with other prophetic intercessors.

Mentoring the Prophetic Intercessor

Once it becomes clear that an intercessor has a prophetic gift, how is this prophetic intercessor to be mentored? Through the

---

[2] A sudden knowledge of a past, present, or future detail without prior knowledge.
[3] An ability to distinguish between a demonic, human, or the Holy Spirit operating in a situation.
[4] An ability to prophesy, by an unction of the Holy Spirit, a word that edifies, comforts, and builds-up the Body of Christ

years I have learned several helpful strategies to assist in both the sharpening of a prophetic gift, as well as developing character and self-discipline. Our two major themes are understanding and embracing God's heart for intercession and also engaging in effective warfare prayer. Interwoven within these two chapters are what I consider to be the foundational biblical values necessary to effectively intercede.

Relating to Church Leadership

One of the fundamental keys to the maturing of a prophetic intercessor has to do with maintaining a healthy connection with the leadership. The truth is these intercessors who *hear God*, need to be in right relationship to leadership. Many pastors find it a challenge to know how to encourage these intercessors, especially if they are uncomfortable or unfamiliar with the prophetic gifts themselves. Nevertheless, it is no mistake that these intercessors are in your congregation or that God has chosen you to be their pastor. If you have trouble relating to prophetic intercessors, let me encourage you that God has placed a special deposit within you that they need. God has also planted a rich deposit in them that is designed to be a blessing to you in addition to the body of Christ. Often pastors have felt inadequate in their ability to understand or relate to intercessors and as a result, avoided them. Intercessors also have been guilty of viewing their leaders as less spiritual if they perceive their leadership as not prophetic. My hope and prayer is that this manuscript will serve as a bridge for pastors and intercessors to recognize and value the role each plays in advancing the kingdom.

A Word to Pastors and Intercessors

What are some of the common misconceptions between pastors and prophetic intercessors? In this chapter I will identify some of these misperceptions and discuss how these two roles were really meant to strengthen one another. Amazingly, much of the problem is due to a lack of instruction in how the other functions and how they are called to interrelate. My intention in addressing some of these issues is to facilitate an understanding that will enable pastors and prophetic intercessors to move past these misconceptions and partner together as God has intended[5].

Launching a Prophetic Prayer Team

How can you establish a prophetic intercession team in your church? Contained within this chapter are some practical insights that I have found useful in this process. As with anything new, what you weave into the initial fabric of a team is crucial to the quality and strength of what is produced. We will explore questions like: What are the things you need to consider in laying the initial foundation to this kind of a prayer team? How do you go about deciding who should be on the team and what criteria do base this on? We will also discuss the importance of establishing a clear vision statement that helps to motivate the on-going prayer focus. Other topics we explore include team building, team dynamics, personal

---

[5] Ephesians 4:16

ministry, team administration and the importance of sabbaticals. All are important factors to consider in developing a successful team.

Establishing a Pastoral Prayer Shield

When I hear of pastors falling into major sin or burning out, the importance of keeping our pastors covered in prayer becomes very clear. We live in a world and in a culture where spiritual leaders are increasingly under spiritual attack. This is why Paul exhorts the church in I Timothy 2:1-2 of the importance of prayer, especially for all those in authority. Another aspect of prophetic intercession involves prayer coverage for the pastoral team. We will focus on how to establish a prayer shield for the pastoral team and answer questions such as: How can you begin to mobilize prayer coverage for the pastoral leadership while maintaining confidentiality? How should this kind of prayer team be administrated? Who should be on this kind prayer team and do they need to be prophetic? We will explore these questions and discuss practical ideas on how to establish this kind of prayer coverage in your church.

Understanding the Role of a Watchman

What is the role of the watchman and what does the watchman watch for? We will discuss this biblical role of the watchman and how part of the responsibility involves praying in agreement with what God has declared prophetically. Most watchmen are prophetic intercessors, but not all prophetic intercessors are necessarily watchmen. I will share insights in understanding the unique position of a watchman and discuss how this role differs from a prophetic intercessor as well as the similarities. We will touch on how watchmen are to connect with the leadership as well as how the prophetic gifts help in this call to stand watch.

Kingdom Advancement and the Benefits of Prophetic Intercession

Prophetic intercession can be of such great value to the local and regional church in so many ways. The heart of a prophetic intercessor as well as the watchman is protective in nature and carries with it an aspect of armor bearing—one who adds strength to those they are called to support. In addition, the prophetic ability to see and to discern enables these intercessors to pray with a Holy Spirit prompted, laser-like precision. This ability to accurately discern and then pray is a powerful tool in not only countering the schemes of the enemy, but also seeing God's purposes established in the earth.

The Journey Begins

"For My thoughts are not your thoughts, neither are your ways My ways," says the Lord. "For as the heavens are higher than the earth, so are My ways higher than your ways and My thoughts than your thoughts."   *Isaiah 55:8-9*

The Prophet had spoken and so the journey began. A week later, I found myself on a mission trip with the three prophesied revelation gifts suddenly becoming active in the form of prophetic dreams, visions, and words of knowledge that I had no clue what to do with! Fortunately, a missionary couple with similar prophetic gifts took me under their wing during those two weeks in Argentina and began to mentor me. They encouraged me to share with them any prophetic sense I had, so they could help me discern what to do with what I perceived.

Ed and Ruth Silvoso had invited me to join them on this mission trip to South America they were hosting in August of 1990. Their team at Harvest Evangelism was mobilizing 120 people from the United States to participate in an evangelistic thrust to reach an entire city in Northern Argentina with the good news of Jesus Christ. This outreach was called *Plan Resistencia.* Cindy Jacobs and Peter and Doris Wagner had gone to Argentina a couple months prior to equip regional pastors and believers with the principles of spiritual warfare and to pray. So when our group from the United States arrived two months later, a lot of the major warfare prayer was already done. I was one of the ground troops sent to evangelize in the second phase of this city-reaching process. I soon realized that I had no idea what I had gotten myself into and seriously wondered if I had missed God on this one!

The spiritual climate in South America is very different from the spiritual climate in the United States. In South America there seems to be a general acceptance of the reality of the spirit realm. Because of this acceptance, spiritual opposition or warfare manifests in more tangible ways than what I had experienced before. In the United States, we are still trying to decide if there are such things as heaven and hell, angels and demons. As I look back now, I see that the Lord had a plan. I was experiencing a crash course in Spiritual Warfare 101 and in a very real sense this was a spiritual boot camp for me in the activation of my prophetic gifts! I will always be grateful for this invitation and the role that Ed and Ruth have played at pivotal junctures in my life. For me, this trip was truly life-changing in my understanding of spiritual warfare, prayer, and God's heart for reaching the lost in cities and nations.

During my time in Argentina, people constantly referred to me as an intercessor. Initially, I resisted that label! At that time, my image of intercessors was of little old ladies who had nothing better to do than to spend hours and hours in prayer. Prayer in the early 1990s was just reemerging as something to be valued in the life of the church. Since that time, I have come to deeply appreciate and admire the older prayer warriors who understood the importance of prayer and were willing to devote their lives to prayer regardless of whether it was popular. I am convinced that the blessings we enjoy today were birthed in prayer closet of those faithful ones!

However, for many years after that mission trip, I continued to struggle with being identified as an intercessor. It seemed that the characteristics of people who were identified as intercessors did not match the way God had made me. Besides, I did not enjoy spending hours and hours in concentrated prayer for a variety of unrelated prayer needs. In addition, when I participated in church-wide (Corporate) prayer during those early days, I used to feel very unspiritual compared to the people who were weeping, wailing, and sincerely pressing into God's purposes. I struggled with feeling very distracted and could not figure out why my prayer experience was so different.

When I did enter into prayer during the unstructured part of a corporate prayer time, it did not take me long to sense a prayer burden, pray the direction I sensed the Lord leading me, and that was it! I was done. So there I was in corporate prayer struggling to think up something else to pray that was not in my spirit and wondering how everyone else could pray for so long! In my feeble attempts to fill up the time, I would belabor the prayer beyond what was really needed or revisit things I had already covered. Yet, my attempts just seemed to irritate me and contribute to why I felt so unspiritual. At times I did experience an extended prayer burden that gave me the unction to pray for a longer time until the burden lifted. However, that usually was not the case!

Something that absolutely amazed me when I did pray was seeing quick answers. The other strange thing I noticed was how the Lord would speak to me when I was not in a prayer mode. Many times I would hear God speak to me when I was driving to work, taking a shower, or just going about my day. Personally, I have discovered that I hear and discern best when I am just going about my day. I have learned that this type of prophetic hearing is due in part to a spiritual gift I function strongly in called the discernment of spirits.

The Beginning Pattern of Prayer

The beginning pattern of prayer for me started when my mother encouraged me, at the age of four, to begin talking to the Lord on my own. As she was tucking me into bed one night, my mother told me I could have a conversation with God anytime I wanted, not just at our nightly prayer time. She told me how Jesus would love to hear all about my day. I was fascinated by my mother's words and a few days later I decided to start my own conversation with Jesus.

I can remember sitting on the floor playing with my toys and telling God how much I really did not like to take naps. How it just did not seem to be fair when I was not tired, especially when it seemed the real reason for my nap was so my mom could have hers! From that day on, I have had ongoing conversations with the Lord throughout my day about anything and everything. Mom *had* said that I could tell Him anything and, being only four, I took her at her word! When I look back now, I am so grateful for my mother's simple instruction to me that night because it began to chart an important course into my future.

Years later, I realized that the pattern my mother had inspired was an aspect of how to pray unceasingly. Prayer for me began in sharing all that was in my heart with Jesus. As I grew older, I realized that if I would take time to listen, He had a few things to say to me too! My childlike understanding of prayer was rooted in these initial conversations with the Lord.

The first time I heard the term *intercessor*, I really did not know how to relate to that word. What did intercession have to do with prayer or my conversations with God?

From Prayer to Intercession

With the introduction of this new word came an understanding of another aspect of prayer that God was showing me. *Intercession* means to petition God on behalf of someone else or a situation. Of course I had always included other people in my prayers, but what it really meant to intercede had me curious. I saw in scriptures how Jesus was called the great intercessor and how He continually intercedes before the Father on our behalf (Hebrews 7:25). When you think of it, what an amazing ongoing prayer support we have. However, my overwhelming question was this: Could Intercession be an aspect of prayer in which Jesus wanted me to follow in His example? The obvious answer was YES!

In the early days of moving into intercession, I discovered an increased desire to pray for my church. In fact, sometimes I just could not wait to get home from work just to have some uninterrupted time in this new aspect of prayer. In the mid-1980s I was living in Vermont and attending a Spirit-filled church. From time to time, as I would sense a burden to pray for the church, the Lord would give me a scripture or an impression of an important direction to pray. Sometimes I felt a prompting to share this impression with my senior pastor, Rick Callahan. I was fortunate enough to have a pastor who was always very gracious with what I shared. Many times, the Lord used Pastor Rick to confirm and encourage me that what I was prophetically sensing was correct.

It was an important time of learning to hear the voice of the Lord. When I did have a prophetic thought, impression, or a scripture that I felt was from the Lord, I was always amazed how the Lord arranged my circumstances to confirm that I was hearing His voice. These confirmations came in many different ways. Sometimes a confirmation came through the message my pastor preached on Sunday morning. Other times, the Lord brought confirmation through a scripture, conversations with other prophetic friends or even through the circumstances in my own life. With each confirmation, there was always an inner peace that I indeed had heard the Lord. I never needed to go in search of a confirmation; the Lord always brought it to me. I have found that God always is faithful to confirm what He is speaking to His people.

From Intercession to Prophetic Intercession

During my mission trip to Argentina in 1990, I found the release of the prophetic gifts was dramatically changing how I prayed. When I would pray for a person or situation, the Lord started to reveal knowledge of what was happening in that person's life that I had no natural way of knowing. This knowledge helped me know how to better target my prayers. Of course understanding what to do with this knowledge did not happen all at once. It was a process.

The first time I received a word of knowledge was on this mission trip and I was just turning in after a long day. I was tired and was not expecting to do anything but sleep. When my head hit the pillow, I heard the voice of the Lord say, "There is a Judas in the ranks." My first reaction was, "What do you mean there is a Judas in the ranks?" This phrase was not familiar to me nor was it a normal speaking pattern for me. I wondered what it meant.

The next day at lunch I shared this word of knowledge with the intercessory leaders. Their initial response was that it was no big deal; there is always a Judas in the ranks. Because they did not seem too concerned, I dismissed the thought as well.

The following morning I was very tired and decided to skip the morning activities. When I rejoined the team at lunch, a woman came running up to me and said, "Wow, that word you gave to the intercessory leader yesterday was really right on!"

Confused, I said, "What are you talking about?"

Unknown to me, this woman had overheard my conversation with the intercessory leader the day before. Then that morning, while I was resting, the leader of the mission trip had made an announcement to the group. There were 120 of us from the United States in addition to 150 Argentine nationals in attendance. The announcement was a confrontation in which the leader said that someone on the trip had come to specifically pray against the success of the trip. The leader said that he knew who it was and that the guilty person needed to come forward. If they were unwilling to do so, then they would be approached by the leadership.

Later, it was confirmed that someone from the United States had come on the trip with the intention of praying against the success of the trip. That is why the woman was so excited to see me. As she told the details of what had happened in the meeting, the Lord was faithful in using her to confirm to me that I had heard His voice!

The Discernment of Spirits

Of the three spiritual gifts that were imparted to me in 1990, the discernment of spirits emerged as the strongest and affected the direction of my prayers the most. Sometimes I would suddenly be aware of a particular demonic spirit that was causing a hindrance or bondage. At first, I did not know what to do with my perception or even how to tell others what I was discerning. I just knew that I had encountered an evil spirit and knew what I felt when I did. Later, I discovered what I sense about a spirit is a major clue in beginning to discern which spirit it is and how it operates. For example, in discerning a spirit of heaviness, I often feel a weight on my emotions or an oppressing spirit in the atmosphere that I just cannot seem to escape. A spirit of fear can feel emotionally overwhelming, especially when we are challenged with difficult circumstances. Fear unleashes a bombardment of lies to make us think things are worse than they really are. It is a spirit that attempts to create a false sense of gloom and hopelessness.

The emergence of this gift came with a heightened sense of awareness of the spiritual realm. When a person is speaking, I can usually discern whether there is the presence of God resting on their words, a demonic influence, or if they are speaking out of their own human spirit. This heightened spiritual awareness also allows me to walk into a room and sense the spiritual climate immediately.

There is a distinct difference between someone who prophesies about a demonic spirit's presence through the gift of prophecy versus the discernment of spirits. With discernment, what I sense or see in the spirit realm usually has a *feeling* aspect to it that has nothing to do with my emotions. For example, if I discern a spirit of confusion, I also sense it. I feel it in the atmosphere around me. I can also discern when an evil spirit has left. Someone with a gift of prophecy may prophesy what the spirit of God is revealing to them about a particular spirit, but not actually sense it themselves.

The pattern that I am about to describe to you is the way God has specifically trained me in this gift of discernment. Maybe others have had a different experience, but this is the pattern that the Lord has brought me through repeatedly. First, I would sense an evil spirit but not necessarily be able to identify it. I would just be aware of its presence and over a period of time I would discern it again and again in different situations. Then, the Lord would begin to reveal and confirm the identity of the spirit and help me to identify clues that I would sense or feel when I was discerning it.

When I first began to discern a Leviathan spirit, also known as the spirit of pride[6], I noticed certain characteristics with each encounter. One of the characteristics was a strong confusion around the people being affected. This confusion made it very difficult to discern the true source of attack. The first few times I encountered this demonic spirit, I was in Argentina. The warfare was very strong and when I would experience this spirit's opposition, it felt like I had been sucker-punched. It was as if the assault came out of nowhere and I felt very disorientated and did not know how to respond. Part of my disorientation came from the impact on my emotions that tempted me to feel insecure and misunderstood. The main goal for this kind of spiritual opposition is to cause division in relationships—usually through a twisting of words. The emotional impact of the misunderstandings that come from this twisting, and the confusion around it, make it very difficult to see that it is a spiritual attack. It just looks like relational problems.

Here is an example of how a Leviathan spirit can influence two people. One time, my sister and I were talking and then began to argue. As we argued, I noticed that we were arguing about what we thought the other person had said. So I called a time out and said, "Do you realize that you are upset with me because you believe I said something that I am telling you I did not say?" The same was true with me; I was upset with

---

[6] Job 41:34

something that I thought I was hearing my sister say, but she wasn't. This misunderstanding became our argument.

When we realized the ridiculousness of the situation, we stopped and prayed. We took authority over the spirit trying to divide us and the attack stopped. In praying we both needed to humble ourselves, admit that we were hearing each other incorrectly, and were making an assumption about what we thought the other meant rather than what was actually said. Sometimes we think we hear what people are saying, but in truth sometimes we are hearing through a filter of our own feelings, thoughts, and pain. This filter skews our ability to hear accurately. When there are unhealed hurts and wounds in our lives, they can potentially become an open door for the enemy to infiltrate our relationships. This is the reason it is important, as Christians, to walk in the biblical principles of love and forgiveness.

Another aspect I began to learn in the discernment process is this: Just because you can identify a particular demonic spirit does not mean you have the wisdom or the release of the Lord to properly deal with it. When the Lord enables you to discern a spirit, then ask the Lord what to do next. It is especially important to ask the Lord what to do when you encounter principalities—ruling spirits that are a primary demonic influence over a city or a nation. In time, the Lord will give you wisdom how to respond when you are confronted with a particular demonic spirit.

As I have matured, I have learned to watch for the effect as well as characteristic patterns of how a demonic spirit is manifesting. Then I ask the Lord for wisdom in how to respond or *if* I need to respond. When I am clear on the direction of the Lord, I pray in agreement with what the Lord wants. Many times the Lord will give me more clarity as I pray. Sometimes warfare prayer may involve binding and loosing, rebuking a demonic spirit, praying the opposite effect of a demonic spirit in a situation, or simply declaring aloud a particular scripture. At times the Lord will give me a word of knowledge about what may give a spirit a legal right to operate in a person's life or situation. Usually a word of wisdom follows in knowing how to pray so the person is freed from this demonic influence. Let me reemphasize the importance of God, as our source of wisdom, in knowing how to respond to any spiritual warfare situation.

I have made it a practice to pay more attention to the spiritual activity of how God is moving rather than what the devil may be doing. Remember, the devil has been competing with God for attention ever since sin entered into Satan's heart and he was cast out of heaven.

"How you are fallen from heaven, O Lucifer, son of the morning! How you are cut down to the ground, you who weakened the nations! For you have said in your heart: 'I will ascend into heaven, I will exalt my throne above the stars of God; I will also sit on the mount of the congregation on the

farthest sides of the north; I will ascend above the heights of the clouds, I will be like the Most High.'"   *Isaiah 14:12-14*

It is clear from this passage Satan desires the worship that rightfully belongs to God alone. The devil is a usurper. Sometimes the most effective warfare is to simply keep your eyes focused on the Lord Jesus and add your faith to the promises God has declared through the written Word (logos) or prophesied. Why is this true? It is because Satan would love to convince us that he is more in control of our circumstances than God. So the enemy's first step in getting your attention is in tempting you to take your eyes off the Lord. In doing so it becomes a vulnerable place where the enemy can deceive you in your mind with unrelenting thoughts of doubt, fear, inadequacy, and hopelessness. This diabolical plan is also designed to attack your emotions to convince you not to trust the Lord in seeing God's promises fulfilled.

The Power of Agreement

Another important reason to keep the correct focus is that God desires for us to partner with Him in accomplishing His kingdom purposes. When we stand in agreement with God and His will, there is a divine connection between the things done in heaven to then be established on the earth.

"Assuredly, I say to you, whatever you bind on earth will be bound in heaven, and whatever you loose on earth will be loosed in heaven. Again I say to you that if two of you agree on

earth concerning anything that they ask, it will be done for them
by my Father in heaven." Matthew 18:18-19

It is important to understand that the enemy is absolutely terrified of the power contained in this agreement! In Matthew 18, the scripture reveals the potential power released through our words, especially when there is an agreement between two people. Just think of the power unleashed when we agree with God's will! One of the most powerful weapons we have in our warfare arsenal is the prayer of agreement when you know God's will about a matter. When we stand in agreement with the Word of God, whether it is in written form, a Rhema Word[7], or through a prophetic utterance[8], it has the supernatural power to accomplish all that God purposed in sending it. The Word not only has the creative power to cause something to be established, but also it has the power to push back the powers of darkness opposing it.

"So is my Word that goes out from my mouth: It will not return
to me empty, but will accomplish what I desire and achieve the
purpose for which I sent it." Isaiah 55:11 (NIV)

A good illustration of the creative power contained in the Word of God is the story of creation found in the book of Genesis.

"Then God said, 'Let there be light'; and there was light."
Genesis 1:3

---

[7] When God speaks through the scriptures (Logos) a now Word for a current situation.
[8] A form of prophecy that is spoken.

Here we see the power of God to create something from nothing. We need to recognize, when God sends his Word, He is issuing a command that has the creative power contained in the Word to call something into being. Everything in the heavens and the earth, all created things, must come into alignment with the issuing of this Word.

"Then God said, 'Let us make man in Our image, according to Our likeness; let them have dominion over the fish of the sea, over the birds of the air, and over the cattle, over all the earth and over every creeping thing that creeps on the earth.'"

Genesis 1:26

We need to understand that God has made man in His image and given him authority in the earth. One aspect of God's likeness is that when we speak, power is released.

"Death and life are in the power of the tongue. And those who love it will eat its fruit."   *Proverbs 18:21*

In other words, there is a consequence, or fruit, that comes from how we speak. If we speak negative things about our lives, our words have the power to create a negative atmosphere around us that really is an agreement with the devil's will about us. This agreement gives the devil a legal right, called a foothold[9], from which to harass us. There is an opposite result when our confession is one of faith. As we know, faith is pleasing to God and so the atmosphere faith

---

[9] Webster's Dictionary defines a foothold as a position usable as a base for advancement.

creates is one in which the power of God can move freely. With this in mind, think how much more powerful our words are when we are prophetically declaring God's will about a situation! The power of agreement is foundational to understanding prophetic intercession. Agreement is the fundamental operating principle to prophetic prayer. This is because prophetic prayer is rooted in discerning the mind of the Lord and then agreeing with Him[10].

From Prophetic Intercessor to Watchman

After several years of learning more about how my prophetic gifts worked, I began to hear the term *watchman* in relationship to prayer. I was curious. So I attended a conference in 1995 in Colorado Springs that began to describe the call of Watchman in the body of Christ. As I listened, I felt a clear understanding of how a watchman watches and prays. I knew instantly that I was called to be a watchman[11].

One aspect to my gift of discernment I never fully understood was an ability to discern the spiritual atmosphere around a person, a place, and even over a region. Often as I am driving in a car, I can discern the spiritual climate over a specific area and even discern a spiritual change in the atmosphere as I drive from city to city or across county lines. That is when I began to distinguish the differences between a prophetic intercessor and a watchman.

---

[10] Reference Chapter 3
[11] Reference Chapter 10

Although a watchman functions in the same spiritual gifts as a prophetic intercessor, watchmen are graced with an ongoing discernment of the spiritual climate over a church or a region.[12] This prophetic sense is a primary result of the gift of the discernment of spirits. If you look in Isaiah 62:6-7, the job of a watchman is linked with what God desires to accomplish in the earth. The assignment to be a watchman may be the result of a prophetic word that has yet to be fulfilled or through the church vision God has revealed to the leadership. This prophetic fulfillment is this reason the watchman is called to stand watch!

In Conclusion

Prayer began for me in simple conversations with God. As I learned to hear His voice and discover burdens the Lord carries on His heart, I discovered another dimension of prayer—intercession. As the prophetic gifts were released in me and then activated in intercession, I began to understand how prophetic prayer serves as a type of armor and protection for the church. Protection comes because of the intercessors' ability to see, hear, and discern the spiritual realm prophetically as they keep watch. Those called to a spiritual watch usually have an ongoing spiritual sense of the spiritual activity over a church or geographical area that can expose and counter the schemes of the enemy. When a watchman is properly submitted to leadership, they become part of a protective

---

prayer shield that can be a tremendous source of prophetic confirmation and insight to pastors as they lead the church. In the upcoming chapters, I will further define what prophetic intercession is and how the kingdom of God advances through prophetic intercession. Although, it is important to understand that all aspects of prayer and intercession are important elements of effective ministry, my primary focus will be on the prophetic aspect of intercession.

Chapter 1

What is Prophetic Intercession Anyway?

"But the manifestation of the Spirit is given to each one for the profit of all: for to one is given the word of wisdom through the Spirit, to another the word of knowledge through the same Spirit, to another faith by the same Spirit, to another gifts of healings by the same Spirit, to another the working of miracles, to another prophecy, to another discerning of spirits, to another different kinds of tongues, to another the interpretation of tongues."   *1 Corinthians 12:7-10*

Prophetic Intercession is a relatively new phrase among Christians. For a long time, anything having to do with intercession was lumped together under the word *prayer*. We now know that there are many different expressions in prayer depending on a person's spiritual gift and prayer burden.

One expression of prayer is what we call a *prophetic intercessor*. The very words *prophetic* and *intercessor* define a specific type of prayer expression. The word *prophetic* has a connotation of one who seeks after and hears God. The word *intercessor* means one who petitions God on behalf of another person or for a situation. Put these two terms together and you have someone who hears God on behalf of someone else and prays in agreement with God's will for the situation[13]. The prayer of agreement with God is the fundamental key to understanding the intercessory flow of a prophetic intercessor.

The Revelation Gifts

Someone who is called a prophetic intercessor usually has at least *one* of the following four revelation gifts[14] operating in their intercessory expression. The gifts are the word of knowledge, the word of wisdom, the discernment of spirits, and prophecy. These are the four gifts of the Holy Spirit through which God reveals something to a person that cannot be known by any natural understanding. This revelation can happen in the context of ministering to another person in prayer, during a prayer meeting, or even while praying on your own. This insight comes from God in the form of knowledge, wisdom, discernment, or a word of prophecy. The purpose for this insight is to bring edification in ministering the Lord's heart in a situation. The following is a short description of the basic function for each gift.

Word of Knowledge: It is the sudden knowledge of a past, present, or future fact about a particular person or situation without any prior knowledge. When this gift is working, it is clear that only the Lord could have revealed the fact or understanding.

---

[13] See Barbara Wentroble's book on *Prophetic Intercession*
[14] I Corinthians 12:7-10

Word of Wisdom: It is a sudden knowing of God's wisdom in a situation for either how to pray for the prayer need or what actions to take. I think of this gift as *knowledge applied.* The key characteristic to a word of wisdom is having a clear sense of direction. Many times the word of knowledge and the word of wisdom work together, much like a tag team. The word of knowledge reveals information not previously known; the word of wisdom reveals what to do with that knowledge or what direction to pray.

Discernment of Spirits: This is the ability to discern the difference between the Spirit of God, a demonic spirit, or the human spirit working in a situation. With this gift is also a heightened sense of the spiritual realm and an ability to discern or identify a particular demonic spirit. Accompanying this seer-type[15] of gift is also an ability to sense or even see demonic or angelic activity.

The Gift of Prophecy: This is an ability to prophesy, by the unction of the Holy Spirit, some past, present, or future event which brings encouragement, comfort, and edification to the Body of Christ.

"But he who prophesies speaks edification and exhortation and comfort to men."   *1 Corinthians 14:3*

In addition, prophetic intercessors often have prophetic dreams, visions, or impressions. They may receive specific

---

[15] A person with an ability to see and discern prophetically.

prayer strategies or sense a *Rhema* word. The following are some of the prophetic expressions people have experienced.

Prophetic Expressions

Visions: A vision is a picture or a series of pictures we see in our mind that reveal a message from the Lord[16]. Some visions may be as simple as seeing a single word over someone's life that shows what God wants to do or bring into a person's life. Many times, with a vision comes a sense of what the Lord is communicating. Some visions are in color and others in black and white. It is important to pay attention to the setting, symbols, colors, actions, words spoken or seen, and the feeling associated with a vision. They are the significant details to understand what God is revealing.

A vision can be like seeing an outdoor scene. For example, suppose that while you are praying for someone, you see a picture of a green forested area with a stream of water gently cascading over small stones. There is a strong feeling of peace with this vision.

In the vision of the forest, the color green is a symbol of life or new life. Trees can represent a place of shelter, while water symbolizes the presence and flow of the Holy Spirit. The feeling of peace experienced in the vision is also an indicator of what the Lord is speaking. In this case, God may be revealing how

---

[16] Acts 10:9-16

he desires to bring rest and renewed strength through a fresh infilling of the Holy Spirit in a person's life.

Another type of vision is an open vision. This happens when someone is fully awake, and what you are seeing in the natural is actually a vision. The following scripture is a good example of an open vision.

"When the servant of the man of God got up early the next morning and went outside, there were troops, horses, and chariots everywhere. 'Ah, my Lord, what will we do now?' he cried out to Elisha. 'Don't be afraid!' Elisha told him. 'For there are more on our side than on theirs!' Then Elisha prayed, 'Oh Lord, open his eyes and let him see!' The Lord opened his servant's eyes, and when he looked up, he saw that the hillside around Elisha was filled with horses and chariots of fire."

II Kings 6:15-17 (NIV)

When Elisha's servant saw the vast army around them, he became fearful and unsure what to do. The servant's perspective was limited to the natural realm. Recognizing this, Elisha prayed that God would open the eyes of his servant to see the truth of the situation from a spiritual vantage point. So God gave Elisha's servant an open vision, where he could see both the natural and the spiritual realm at the same time, to dispel his fear.

Dreams: Dreams are really visions experienced while sleeping and are interpreted in the same way as visions.[17] A dream from God can be one of warning, direction, discernment, or encouragement[18]. Not all dreams are sent from God and dreams need to be judged carefully, but dreams are a very common way that God communicates to His people.

One night I dreamed that I was riding in the back seat of a car that was traveling from my home to the church, twelve miles away. On the freeway, I noticed that the weather was overcast and cloudy. It looked like we were traveling through a storm. I looked out the left window and noticed a vague purple color beginning to appear in the air near the car. As I continued to stare at this color, the thought occurred to me that this could be the beginning of a rainbow. What began as a vague color suddenly burst into a rainbow with an arch overhead and the ends of the rainbow on either side of the car. I remember thinking how vibrant the colors were.

As the car continued down the freeway, another rainbow sprang forth from the right door of the car as we passed a certain spot on the road. Out my left window, I could see another rainbow suddenly appear in the distance ahead. As I turned to the right, I saw another rainbow in the shape of an oval set in a white cloud. I could see a brilliant white light in the center of the rainbow. I thought this was so unusual that a

---

[17] See above section on visions
[18] See Matthew 1:20-24; Matthew 2:12

rainbow would be set in the clouds like that and pondered the reason. I had the sense that the presence of the Lord and spiritual breakthrough was connected with the cloud. Then, I realized it was the fourth rainbow I had seen. Although it was not raining in my dream, I was aware that the sun must be shining from behind me for these rainbows to be appearing.

When I woke up from this dream, I had a very clear sense that the Lord was about to cause His promises to be fulfilled for both me and my church. I had the impression that the promises were beyond just a personal application because the rainbows appeared between my house and the church. I understood these rainbows were prophetic words or promises that we had received individually and as a congregation. A rainbow in scripture symbolizes God's promise.

I felt the Lord was saying to me through this dream that the season we had been in was like moving through a storm—a season of difficulty and spiritual opposition. But as we continued to move forward along His chosen path for our lives, represented by the highway, the Lord would break through in the midst of the storm to fulfill His promises. The circular rainbow symbolized to me the presence of the Lord bringing a spiritual breakthrough. In the dream, I understood the multiple rainbows represented the promises that God causes to suddenly spring forth in our lives at an appointed time. At the time I had this dream, our church was going through a period of spiritual opposition because we were standing in faith for the fulfillment of some prophetic promises. The dream was a great encouragement to me and others when I shared it.

Impressions: Impressions are the effect of the Holy Spirit causing a prophetic thought to be impressed upon your spirit. Impressions are not as clear as dreams or visions; they are more a vague sensing of what the Lord is communicating. There may be a visual aspect to an impression where you see a vague image in your mind's eye. Impressions can also be a type of spiritual sensing that discerns the direction of how the Lord is moving in a prophetic sense.

One time I had an impression that was also a partial vision while I was praying for a friend. During my prayer for her, I saw the letters *REV* in a vision. Although I only saw the first three letters, I also had an impression, or a sense, that the rest of the letters spelled the word "revelation." When I asked the Lord what this meant, He gave me an instant understanding. God was about to bring revelation to an area of my friend's life, but not all at once—it would be progressive over time. That is why I only saw the first three letters in the vision. God was revealing his message through how the vision appeared to me. I believe the Lord gave this picture to me because He wanted to encourage my friend in what He was about to do.

Rhema Word: This is when God speaks through his written Word as a current Word of revelation to that individual[19]. Often,

---

[19] Matthew 4:4

people receive a Rhema Word when they are reading the scriptures. Usually they say things like this, "I was reading along and a verse just jumped off the page at me and I knew God was speaking to me through that passage." They may have read this same verse many times before, but this time it became a fresh revelation. Another way a Rhema Word can come is when the Lord reminds you of a scripture that speaks an understanding to your current circumstance[20]. Many times in prayer the Lord has reminded me of a scripture that has been a vital Word for a current situation.

The Song of the Lord: The Song of the Lord is a prophetic expression that is strongly connected to a musical expression of worship. Psalms, hymns, and spiritual songs are encouraged forms of praise and worship in both the Old and New Testament. Spiritual songs are unusual in that they are spontaneously prompted by the Lord as a response to God's presence. In the Old Testament, Psalm 33:3 exhorts Israel to *sing to Him a new song.* This new song has to do with a spontaneous expression of worship sung by dedicated believers as a form of worship to God. Where does this worship take place? The Bible reveals in Psalms how Israel was exhorted to sing a new song among the believers.

"Praise the Lord! Sing to the Lord a new song, and His praise in the congregation of the godly ones."　　　　*Psalm 149:1 (NLT)*

---

[20] John 14:26

In the New Testament, Paul calls the expression of spontaneous new songs as singing spiritual songs.

"Let the word of Christ dwell in you richly in all wisdom, teaching and admonishing one another in psalms and hymns and spiritual songs, singing with grace in your hearts to the Lord."   *Colossians 3:16.*

When the word of God is dwelling richly in a person, one of the expressions of the inner working of His word is that the Holy Spirit will prompt someone, in both words and melody, to sing a song of praise and worship to Him. This happens because His Spirit lives within us. When the Holy Spirit prompts a person to sing, the Holy Spirit becomes the author of the song. We are merely His vessel through which this song is expressed.

From a time of praise and worship often comes what is called the *Song of the Lord.* This song is a prophetic message God communicates to His people. Instead of being spoken, the Song of the Lord is a prophecy that is sung for the purpose of edifying, building-up, and encouraging the Body of Christ.[21] The Song of the Lord can be sung in one's own language or in a prophetic tongue and typically occurs in the worship portion of a service.

"For if I pray in a tongue, my spirit prays, but my understanding is unfruitful. What is the conclusion then? I will pray with the

---

[21] 1 Corinthians 14:3-4

Spirit, and I will also pray with the understanding. I will sing with the spirit and I will also sing with understanding."

1 Corinthians 14:14-15

Prophetic Dance: When the Spirit of the Lord touches a person, sometimes he or she may respond in a prophetic dance. Prophetic dance can be a type of warfare in defeating the enemy through worship as a declaration of victory[22]. Like other prophetic gifts, this kind of dance is initiated by a prompting of the Holy Spirit.

Once I saw a woman at church enter into this kind of prophetic dance. As I walked into the church sanctuary, I noticed a woman worshiping alone. She was so caught up in worship that she did not notice I entered the room. Then I noticed her begin to dance before the Lord. As she moved up and down the aisles, the Lord began to give me understanding of what He was doing while she danced. Her very steps were like an act of warfare in defeating the enemy's schemes. It was like watching warfare prayer being acted out rather than verbalized. As the woman continued dancing, I was amazed at the victory I sensed in my spirit as well as a strong presence of the Lord in the room.

Prophetic Acts: These are physical acts of faith, done in the natural, to agree with what God is revealing in the supernatural realm[23]. A prophetic act can be simply joining hands with other

---

[22] Psalm 30:11; 2 Samuel 6:14-15
[23] Numbers 20:8-11

believers as a sign of how God desires to bring greater unity to the Body of Christ. Usually a prophetic act begins as a word of wisdom. The Holy Spirit then prompts a physical action that can be done to reflect this revelation. The act is a form of agreement. An Old Testament example of a prophetic act is in Jeremiah 19:10-11.

"Then you shall break the flask in the sight of men who go with you, and say to them, 'Thus says the Lord of hosts: Even so I will break this people and this city, as one breaks a potter's vessel, which cannot be made whole again; and they shall bury them in Tophet till there is no place to bury."

Although this is a sobering word, it is a clear picture how a physical action can illustrate a prophetic word. It is a prophetic act. In this case, it was used as a sign of impending judgment.

Please exercise restraint in the use of prophetic acts by not turning every revelation into a prophetic act. Making every revelation into a prophetic act is an overuse of what should be a spontaneous prompting of the Holy Spirit.

Prophetic Strategies: These strategies come from a word of wisdom. They are a sudden understanding of how something should be done to get victory. The books of Nehemiah and Esther are good examples of the Lord exposing the plans of the enemy and revealing a specific strategy to counter these threats[24]. Another biblical example of a prophetic strategy is

---

[24] Nehemiah 4:7-16;Esther 4-8

found in the fall of Jericho[25]. In this account, Joshua arrives at Jericho only to find the gates of the city shut and no one allowed in or out.

"But the Lord said to Joshua, 'I have given you Jericho, its king, and all its mighty warriors. Your entire army is to march around the city once a day for six days. Seven priests will walk ahead of the Ark, each man carrying a ram's horn. On the seventh day you are to march around the city seven times, with the priests blowing the horns. When you hear the priests give one long blast on the horns, have all the people give a mighty shout. Then the walls of the city will collapse, and the people can charge straight into the city."   *Joshua 6:2-6 (NLT)*

The effectiveness of such a strategy depends on a willingness to obey the Lord. I am sure Joshua and his army did not understand how walking around a city for seven days could possibly change their situation. Even more puzzling was the shout to be given on the seventh day—how could this cause the walls of a fortified city to crumble? We may not always understand the reasons why God leads us to do things in a certain way, but what is clear is how obedience is essential! A prophetic shout released at an appointed time is a powerful weapon in defeating the enemy as the battle of Jericho showed.

Another important strategy is prayer and fasting. In Matthew 17:21, the disciples are asking why they could not cast a

---

[25] Joshua 6

demon out of an epileptic boy. Jesus tells them it is because an additional strategy is needed in casting out this kind of demon. He identifies the missing ingredient as prayer and fasting.

Prophetic strategies are a valuable source of God's wisdom and insight. The benefit of receiving God's wisdom is in knowing what to do as well as when to do it. So often we rely on our own understanding rather than seeking the counsel of the Lord for the battles we face or for the spiritual progress we desire. The book of Joshua reveals that Israel experienced miraculous victories when they sought the Lord for His wisdom to drive out the inhabitants of their promised land. We can also see the trouble Israel encountered in failing to seek the Lord[26]. Seeking the mind and counsel of the Lord is an important principle that can actually propel us into the realm of the miraculous to accomplish His kingdom purposes. There is a consistent pattern throughout scripture[27] of supernatural events occurring when a people are willing to do things God's way. It all begins with prayer!

Prophetic Art: Artists who are inspired of the Holy Spirit may feel a prophetic unction to communicate, through drawings or paintings, a prophetic message of what God is doing. When others look at prophetic art, they may feel blessed as they perceive the presence of the Lord in the art. What is drawn or

---

[26] Joshua 9:3-24
[27] Genesis 7; Exodus 7,14,16 and 17; Joshua 3, 6, 8

painted often resonates within a person's spirit a message that God is speaking to them.

I have been in a few conferences where Christian artists have been allowed to paint during the worship time of the service. At one conference, I had the privilege of observing a prophetic artist closely. It was evident, with every brush stroke, that the painting was an act of expressing heart-felt worship. Even the use of certain colors revealed how this artist's spirit interpreted what he discerned to be images of God's glory. When the painting was done, I was amazed at how the painting inspired me. In the artwork of other prophetic artists I have found inspiration is a common characteristic.

Tongues and the Interpretation of a Tongue: There are times when God will release a prophetic word to the Body of Christ through the gift of tongues. Instead of a whole group of people praying in tongues at the same time, this type of prophecy is spoken out by just one person. Usually when one person speaks in a tongue either that person or another person can interpret this prophetic word so that the Body of Christ can have understanding[28].

Once when I was a teenager, the Holy Spirit prompted me to give a prophecy in a tongue. I had gone over to my friend Debbie's home. We were new Christians and had been learning about the gifts of the Holy Spirit. For some reason, we decided to spend some time in prayer. While praying, I had a

---

[28] 1 Corinthians 14:5, 15

strong unction to begin praying in a tongue. As I did, something was different from the other times I had prayed in my prayer language. It was like speaking a message that had a starting and ending point. I think I only spoke for about ten to fifteen seconds. I had been taught a few months earlier that a prophecy in tongues needed an interpreter. I started to feel a little concerned because Debbie and I were the only people in the room and we were not exactly experts. The prophecy had come as a complete surprise. So now what? Just as my concern was turning into panic, I heard Debbie give an interpretation. She spoke in a similar pattern with a starting point and a clear ending point for the same duration as when I spoke. The only difference was that she spoke in English. When she finished, we both knew God had been speaking to us! Although I do not remember the prophecy fully, I do remember that the Lord was assuring us that He was watching over and guiding us like little lambs.

The chart listed below shows some of the prophetic expressions that flow out of the four revelation gifts. It is important to note that a vision can be categorized as a word of wisdom, word of knowledge, discernment of spirits, or prophecy. It depends on the nature of what is being revealed. Although the chart may not include every prophetic expression, the chart is meant to show how the prophetic expressions can flow from the four revelation gifts. Other prophetic expressions may stem from one or two prophetic gifts. For example, the

Song of the Lord and Prophetic Dance tend to flow mostly from the gift of prophecy. Prophetic acts and prayer strategies mostly involve the word of wisdom because they characteristically express a sense of the Lord's direction (see the Spiritual Gifts chart on the next page).

A Different Prayer Flow

Generally speaking, I have found that many prophetic intercessors struggle with identifying themselves as an *intercessor*. It is not because they do not value prayer or intercession. It is because of the old stereotypes associated with being an intercessor. Another reason for this struggle can come from how prophetic intercessors flow in prayer. The flow of prophetic intercessors is very different from other praying people. It is not better, just different.

This difference between prophetic intercessors and other praying people comes from the fact that the revelation gifts are activated as a precursor to praying in the direction the Lord reveals. On a prayer team of prophetic intercessors, the goal of prayer is to cover one issue at a time rather than many. This goal allows prophetic revelation to come forth so that intercessors can pray with insight for a particular situation. Prophetic intercessors watch for what God is doing in a situation, or wants to do, and then they pray in agreement.

There is a good illustration of this principle in the book of John:

SPIRITUAL GIFTS CHART

Prophetic Expressions	Revelation Gifts			
	Word of Knowledge	Word of Wisdom	Discernment of Spirits	Prophecy
Dreams	X	X	X	X
Visions	X	X	X	X
Rhema Word	X	X	X	X
Impressions	X	X	X	X
Song of the Lord		X		X
Prophetic Dance				X
Prophetic Acts		X		
Prophetic Strategies		X		X
Prophetic Art				X
Tongues and Interpretation of a Tongue		X		X

"Then the Jesus answered and said to them, 'Most assuredly, I say to you, the son of God can do nothing of Himself, but what He sees the Father do; for whatever He does, the son also does in like manner."   *John 5:19*

Jesus only did what he saw the Father doing. As Jesus discerned what the Father was doing, he did likewise. Here is a picture of how we are to move in agreement on a prophetic intercessory level. Our prayers should reflect and agree with what we see our heavenly Father doing.

Prophetic intercessors often see how the enemy is hindering the work of God. When that happens, prophetic intercessors should seek God for His wisdom and strategy to combat whatever the devil is doing to hinder the vision or work of God.

Prophetic intercessors also have a strong desire to enter into a prophetic flow with other prophetic intercessors because of the sense of effectiveness and insight received during prophetic prayer. When the spirit of God is strongly moving in a prayer time, hours can go by and it feels like minutes. Many times prophetic intercessors see quick answers or confirmations for their prayers and they experience a great inner peace when they finish. Peace comes because of the sense of accomplishment in having heard the Lord and prayed according to His direction. A sense of accomplishment is one motivating factor for prophetic intercessors.

Corporate Prayer and the Prophetic Intercessor

Although I am a firm believer in corporate prayer—a prayer meeting that is open to the whole congregation—that meeting format can be difficult for prophetic intercessors because of how they are graced to function in prayer. Some corporate prayer settings are a challenge because there is not a clear prayer focus or people are praying what I call spontaneous prayers—where people are encouraged to pray aloud for many different topics. Remember that a prophetic intercessor thrives on hearing the Lord while covering one issue in prayer, not several. When a prayer focus changes quickly, it often causes prophetic intercessors to feel interrupted in their attempts to hear God. Prophetic intercessors want to pray with others who are flowing in the same prophetic direction.

It is not that one kind of prayer is better than another. All kinds of prayers are valuable expressions! However, it is important to understand some distinct differences so that we can better function all together. Over the years, I have known prophetic intercessors who refuse to attend corporate prayer meetings because they cannot find a place for prophetic expression. Many feel they are more effective in their prayers by staying home and praying on their own.

It is my personal belief that a corporate prayer time is an important connecting point for the Body of Christ, regardless of anyone's particular intercessory expression or prayer burden. It is an opportunity to agree together in prayer for what we know

God is revealing and a powerful tool in moving the church forward in a unified vision. The best prophetic intercessors understand the power of agreement quite well because agreement is the underlying current in how they pray.

A way to draw prophetic intercessors together is to structure a corporate meeting with a just a few prayer points. Focused prayer can be done as a large group, with one person praying and the rest standing in agreement, or in small groups of three or four people where each person has an opportunity to pray for the assigned prayer focus. It is a nice compromise for people who are prophetic in their prayer expression and people who are not. Regardless of how leaders organize a corporate prayer time, if they pray for just couple prayer points, it will bring a greater unity and motivation for everyone to pray.

At GateWay City Church, our senior pastor has organized the corporate prayer time to be unstructured for the first hour and a half. People are free to walk around the room, kneel, lie on the floor, or pray in small groups. People can pray aloud or silently, just as long as they are careful to not be disruptive and are sensitive to the level of sound in the room. After the first hour, one of our musicians starts to play worship songs while people continue to pray. During the last half an hour, everyone is called forward to worship and pray in agreement for some things that God has put on the heart of our pastors. Our senior pastor usually leads this prayer time. When he is away, one of the associate pastors leads the focused prayer time.

The format has been effective for us. Over the past 14 years, we have seen many people in our congregation, in addition to our intercessors, attend regularly. On the average, 100 to 150 people attend weekly. That is approximately 15 percent of our congregation.

What makes this corporate prayer time so effective? I think there are four keys. The first and most important key is that our senior pastor asked the Lord for wisdom in how to structure the corporate prayer time. Initially he got a clear sense that our meetings should be from 6 to 8 a.m. on Saturday mornings. He also got a sense of how to organize the time. God may reveal a different strategy to another church. The most important thing is to seek God for His plan and not rely on your own ideas or on how someone else has done something.

The second key is that our pastoral leadership has modeled for the congregation the importance of prayer. The pastors have led by example by making our corporate prayer time a priority to attend themselves. By attending the prayer times, the pastors have imparted a value of prayer that others in the congregation embrace as well.

The third key is that the meeting format allows a freedom of expression for all people who want to pray. A person does not have to be an intercessor, either prophetic or general, to feel comfortable in this setting. People who just like to pray are welcome.

The fourth key to making the prayer time attractive is in the prophetic atmosphere that is created as we agree together in prayer at the end of the meeting. One of our pastors will share an encouraging scripture or a prophetic sense of the direction we are to pray. Such sharing helps to create a sense of spiritual freshness. People usually walk away feeling encouraged and feeling the prayer time was a positive experience.

The people who attend GateWay's corporate prayer time receive benefits because they experience three levels of connection. I call the levels of connection the 3 C's.

1) Connection with the vision of the church: During our times of corporate prayer agreement, the overall prophetic direction is expressed and prayed for. It is a great place for someone who is new to the church to begin to catch the vision and direction of the church.

2) Connection with the Lord: The unstructured part of the prayer meeting is a wonderful time to connect with the Lord personally, in addition to praying for the advancement of God's kingdom purposes through our local church.

3) Connection with other brothers and sisters in Christ: Corporate prayer is also a great opportunity for people to connect with other members of the congregation they might not otherwise see. Many people go out for coffee

or breakfast after the prayer time. It is a natural connection time for people to make new friends, build ministry connections, and enjoy fellowship together.

Ministry Expressions and the Prophetic Intercessor

I believe prayer and prophetic intercession is foundational for all effective ministry. Prayer is the place where we can discern the mind of Christ and receive his wisdom in how to minister.

In addition to prayer groups, a prophetic intercessor can easily fit into various ministry expressions in the local church. In identifying these, am I implying that you have to be prophetic to be effective on these teams? No. Your prayer burden and spiritual gift is given by God and he is pleased with your faithful stewardship of it in whatever ministry He calls you to serve. My purpose in identifying just a few of these is to give you some ideas of ministry opportunities in which a prophetic intercessor could be of great value. Some areas are closely related to a prayer-type of ministry and other areas are ministries in which prophetic intercessors would be a great blessing.

Deliverance Ministry

The most obvious expression for the prophetic gifts is in the area of deliverance. Deliverance is a ministry of praying for Christians to be set free from any demonic influence or generational pattern of bondage. The prophetic gifts are particularly helpful in identifying and exposing what may be holding a person in bondage and discerning when a person has been delivered. The greater significance of this ministry, aside from the personal aspect of freedom, is the spiritual impact to a city or geographical area. Each time a person receives deliverance from an area of bondage, the enemy loses his power to influence. He is displaced. When many people are delivered through a Cleansing Stream retreat, the deliverance ministry we have in our area, it strongly impacts the spiritual climate of a region and enables people to move more fully into all that God has purposed for them. Prophetic intercessors are a tremendous help in the process of deliverance.

If your church is involved in a deliverance ministry within your own church or as a coalition of churches partnering together, it is well worth the time of believers to keep this ministry covered in prayer. I highly recommend that prayer coverage be mobilized in partnership with those involved in this kind of ministry. In our area, we have coordinated prayer among the regional churches when there is an upcoming retreat. These retreats are times when people, who are going through a process of healing and deliverance from generational bondages and sin patterns, can receive help. We are all called to help advance God's kingdom. The deliverance ministry is very effective in extending God's kingdom and appropriating our freedom in Christ.

The Role of an Armor Bearer

Another area of ministry is being a personal armor bearer— someone who has a prayer assignment to cover a leader in ongoing prayer. Armor bearers usually have a God-given prayer burden for a particular leader. These prophetic intercessors have some noteworthy characteristics. Armor bearers usually have a heart with a deep sense of loyalty, protection, servant-hood, and an amazing ability to add strength to the leaders because of their sensitivity to the Holy Spirit to pray targeted prayers. The revelation gifts are used to guard and protect a leader much like a watchman guards the church. Something that deeply grieves the spirit of these intercessors is any talk of disloyalty, murmuring, or complaining about the leader they are covering in prayer. Armor bearers are intensely loyal people who stand guard and protect in prayer the spiritual vision and calling of the leader they are assigned. Many times the Lord graces them with very specific insight in how to pray. Armor bearers instinctively know that their prayer burdens are assigned by God and only feel a relief from their assignments when the Lord brings a release in their spirit.

Prayer for the Nations

Many prophetic intercessors have a heart to pray on a national or international level. These intercessors can receive very strategic prophetic insights. Strategic prayer can be extremely beneficial to a pastor, leader, missionary, or to short-term mission groups when they travel. Because of the revelation gifts, prophetic intercessors can discern if there is any form of opposition and pray very strategically for those traveling, even before anyone gets on an airplane.

Usually when I lead a team in prayer for our pastor, who travels internationally from time to time, we start to pray a day or two before the scheduled trip. By praying in advance, we can begin to discern any spiritual opposition, pray agreement for the set purpose of the trip, and see if the Holy Spirit wants to move in a special way. Our advance prayers prepare the spiritual atmosphere. So when our pastor arrives, we have already gone ahead of him in prayer to push through any spiritual opposition that would try to buffet him or oppose God's divine purpose for that ministry assignment. Advance prayer does not mean that there will not be any warfare. We have also experienced times when we have had to stay on alert, during the time our pastor was gone, because of the opposition he experienced with connecting flights, weather conditions, ground transportation, physical infirmity, spiritual attack at the ministry location, and so on. For major ministry trips—such as ones to Thailand, Indonesia, Cambodia, and Israel—if I sense a greater need for prayer coverage, I will mobilize our church to fast and pray during the time he is away.

Some intercessors may want to pray strictly for nations. They feel a specific burden to pray for the breaking of spiritual bondages over nations so that people are more open to the gospel. Again the level of prophetic discernment can be very strategic. My caution for anyone who prays at this level of prayer is that he or she needs to be under the covering of the pastoral leadership in the local church. Intercessors may discern a principality over a nation, but discernment is not equal to the release of the Lord or the spiritual authority to combat a principality. Kicking a principality off its throne is not the same as keeping it off! Consider the spiritual dynamic of this passage in Matthew.

"When an evil spirit comes out of a man, it goes through arid places seeking rest and does not find it. Then, it says, 'I will return to the house I left.' When it arrives and finds the house unoccupied, swept clean and put in order. Then it goes and takes with it seven other spirits more wicked than itself, and they go to live there. And the final condition of that man is worse than the first."   *Matthew 12:43-45a (NIV)*

The potential harm in praying outside the Lord's will against a principality can mean a demonic re-empowerment that is seven times stronger than the original demon. Consider the impact of this over an entire nation! I believe God has a timetable over geographic areas for the release of this kind of strategic-level warfare in combating principalities. It is very important to discern how God is moving in a geographical area and to stay in alignment with how the Holy Spirit is leading. Unless God divinely intervenes to release the equivalent of a *Great Awakening*, spiritual preparation in the area is needed in order to maintain a regional deliverance that involves a principality. It is vital for intercessors to be properly connected to pastoral or apostolic leadership and to be moving in the right timing for this level of strategic warfare.

The most effective prayers over nations are prayers that discern how God is moving over a particular country and come into agreement with that! If you sense a stronghold over a nation, pray the opposite of the spiritual effects you see impacting the people. For example, the spirit of Jezebel manifests itself with control, manipulation, seduction, witchcraft, discouragement, loss of purpose, and sexual immorality. A good way to intercede is to pray the opposite way this spirit has influenced the thinking of the believers. Ask the Lord to cleanse the church from areas of influence by this spirit. As the church is freed from this kind of influence, this stronghold begins to lose its demonic grip over the area. In part, this is how righteousness can been sown into the land in preparation for strategic-level warfare. As the church walks in a life-style of holiness that is opposite to the demonic influence, the strength of that principality lessens and the church is better able to advance. This kind of ground-level warfare is called *displacement.* Essentially, each time someone receives Jesus as Lord and Savior or experiences personal deliverance, that demonic principality loses its power to influence. The purpose of demonic entities is to blind the minds of people so that they cannot receive the truth.

"Satan, the god of this evil world, has blinded the minds of those who do not believe, so that they are unable to see the glorious light of the Good News that is shining upon them. They

do not understand the message we preach about the glory of Christ, who is the exact likeness of God."

2 Corinthians 4:4 (NLT)

Prayer Journeys

A prayer journey involves taking a team of intercessors, not necessarily just prophetic intercessors, to a city, region, or nation to pray over that geographical area. Although, prophetic intercessors can be very helpful in capturing the prophetic sense of what God is revealing during the journey. Usually a lot of prayer and seeking the Lord has gone in to determining where to go. When there is a clear direction from the Lord, then it is time to assemble a team of people who are willing to make this journey. When our church has done prayer journeys, the prayer assignment has been very simple. We ask the Lord to show us how to pray His heart, at this time, for the city, region or nation we will be traveling to. Some of the places we have gone to are Washington DC; Berlin, Germany; and Israel.

The leadership team for the trip usually directs how, when, and at which site to pray during the prayer journey. Sometimes there may be a strong prophetic sense of what to pray, declare, or what prophetic act to do at a specific location. Other times, we may feel led to pray a simple prayer of blessing. It is helpful to have a general itinerary in place for each day as well as a flexible tour guide and bus driver if the Holy Spirit prompts the re-arrangement of which sites to visit. On our journeys we have experienced many unexpected divine appointments. The unexpected moves of the Holy Spirit always make for an exciting trip. Usually we make a prayer journey every twelve to eighteen months and keep the actual prayer assignment to three or four days. Making a regular prayer journey is a wonderful way to further equip and inspire prayer within the Body of Christ.

Pastoral Prayer Shield

Another valuable expression is on-going prayer coverage for the senior pastor, apostle, and pastoral team. It is so important to keep these faithful servants uplifted. When you think of all the reports of pastors leaving the ministry because they are burned out, discouraged, attacked by infirmity, or falling into sin, I wonder, "How many of those same pastors had on-going prayer coverage with committed intercessors?" The devil is no dummy; he knows that if you strike the shepherd, the sheep scatter[29]. Scattered sheep are then open targets to feeling disillusioned, confused, betrayed, and angry. By driving out the pastor, the enemy can work great havoc within a local church. It is important to realize the attack on the shepherd is really designed to bring harm to the Body of Christ. For the health of the whole body, it is imperative to keep our leadership covered in prayer. Prophetic intercessors serve by praying targeted prayers in support of leadership. Later, we will discuss how to put together an effective prayer shield[30].

---

[29] Zech 13:7
[30] Reference Chapter 9

Spiritual Mapping Team

Spiritual Mapping is the process of discerning what may be blocking the gospel from having a greater impact in a geographical area. Having led a regional mapping team, I can tell you that there are two essential elements to the success of this kind of a team: gifted researchers and prophetic intercessors. The focus for a mapping team is to identify spiritual strongholds that have been established through an historical event, declaration, or cultural tradition. Over time, these ungodly belief systems become established mindsets or cultural identities over geographical areas. The enemy uses spiritual strongholds to blind the minds of people groups from receiving the truth of the gospel.

In our area, Santa Clara County, California, one of the major strongholds affecting the mindset of people is pride—intellectual pride. Pride is the functional name and Leviathan is the proper name for this spirit. Pride says, "I do not need God; I control my own destiny. Everything I have is by my own doing." As a result of research, I can show you how this mindset is a functional pattern of behavior historically as well as in the current spiritual climate.

The ultimate goal for any mapping team always should be to see lost souls saved and transforming revival come to the land. One of the important operating principles for spiritual mapping is this: What you hear from the Lord through prophetic intercession regionally should also confirm a documented historical pattern found in the research. Prophetic intercession and research each should validate the other. Prophetic Intercessors are very helpful in initially identifying spiritual strongholds, seeking God for his strategy in dismantling them, and praying in agreement with how the Lord wants to impact a region.

Watchman for the Local or Regional Church

The role of a watchman includes an aspect of armor bearing. The heart of a watchman is always to guard and protect the work of the ministry and the people of God. A watchman guards and protects others by watching. Pastors, whether or not they are prophetic, are a type of watchman. Like a good shepherd, pastors watch over the sheep to keep the believers protected from wolves who would try to deceive them, lead them astray, and ultimately bring them harm.

A prophetic intercessor in the role of a watchman carries a different responsibility than a pastor. Through the operation of revelation gifts, a prophetic intercessor can discern the movement of the Lord as well as the schemes of the enemy. A prophetic watchman has an awareness of the spiritual climate regionally and discernment of how the spiritual climate may be impacting the local church. This spiritual awareness allows intercessors pray more effectively in response. Prophetic revelation, especially when discerning demonic strategies, should be submitted to the pastoral leadership. It is helpful to designate a liaison between the prophetic intercessors and the church leadership. A liaison, such as a prayer pastor, prayer coordinator, or intercessory leader, can simplify communication about prophetic revelations to the church leadership.

Music Ministry Team

All those involved in music ministry should have an active prayer life as part of their personal preparation process. Prophetic intercessors can play a significant role in the success of the worship time. Praise and worship is a time when the congregation is entering into the presence of the Lord and is preparing to receive the Word. Praise begins the process by invoking the presence of the Lord. As God begins to inhabit the praises of His people, worship follows[31]. Worship is really a response to the presence of God.

Praise and worship are the way God prepares the hearts of His people to receive the ministry of the Holy Spirit during the service. As we enter into God's presence, the power of God is released. When God's power is released, minds are renewed, the prophetic is activated, the voice of the Lord becomes clear, people experience healing, backsliders recommit their lives, and nonbelievers make decisions to receive Christ.

When I was in music ministry, the Lord gave me, and others on the team, wisdom of how to pray strategically during worship. I have seen how the Lord uses praise and worship, together with intercession, to change the spiritual atmosphere over people

---

[31] Psalm 22:3

during a service. There is a unique place of intercession within praise and worship. In this place, I have found prayer to be even more effective and strategic. One time when I was serving on the worship team, the Lord gave me a vision of how spiritual oppression was resting over the congregation we were ministering to. In the vision it looked like a dark cloud. As I prayed and rebuked this oppression, I saw the cloud lift and the light of God's presence break through. It was like an overcast day when the sun finally breaks through. In the vision, I could see the light overtake the darkness. When it happened, I noticed the spiritual atmosphere also had changed. More members of the congregation were worshipping and I could sense a strong presence of the Lord.

Apostolic Ministry Teams

To understand this type of ministry team we must first define the word *apostolic*. This word is derived from the Greek word *apostolos* meaning to send or mission. This expression is mostly used in conjunction with the work of an apostle. From reading Dr. David Cannistraci's book on *Apostles and the Emerging Apostolic Movement*, we learn that there is such a thing as an apostolic people. Dr. Cannistraci defines an apostolic people as "Christians who support and participate in apostolic ministry, but who are not actual apostles"[32]. One characteristic of an apostolic people is that they reflect the characteristics of the apostolic ministry they serve. Because of

---

[32] See page 29 of *Apostles and the Emerging Apostolic Movement*

the strong emphasis of equipping and leadership within most apostolic churches, ministry teams are developed and sent out by an apostolic ministry to support other area churches.

One type of apostolic ministry team is a prophetic intercession team. An apostolic church may see a need or receive a request for personal ministry from the regional churches to which they relate. Another church may need someone to help train and equip them in developing prayer teams. While those who are apostolic are characterized by strong leadership, their heart is always to minister with an attitude of humility and servant-hood in training, equipping, and releasing believers for the work of the ministry.

Counseling Ministry

The revelation gifts, especially words of knowledge and words of wisdom, can be very helpful in biblical counseling situations in getting to the root issue. This is not to say that in order to be a good counselor you have to be prophetic, but it can definitely be a tremendous benefit.

If you do receive a word of knowledge, a good way to present this word is by asking a question. For example, suppose you are in a counseling session and you receive a word of knowledge. This word reveals that the person has a root of bitterness because of their father's harsh treatment of them as a child. First, be sure to discern the release of the Lord in addressing this situation. Then start with a general question, such as, "What is your relationship like with your father?" This is a good way to gauge whether someone is ready to discuss something that may be painful. If you sense openness in the person's response, you might ask, "Do you struggle with bitterness against your father?" If the person does not agree, then stop. Abuse may be something that they are not ready to deal with or are unaware of. Never continue to share a word of knowledge with someone if you see that they are not open to it. You may be wrong in what you have discerned or it is not the right time to share the knowledge.

Other Prayer Teams

Prophetic intercessors do not have to be only with other prophetic intercessors to feel effective. In most prayer groups, home fellowships, and other prayer times there usually are some prophetic intercessors. Prophetic intercessors are the ones, in a prayer setting, who say things, such as, "While I was praying, the Lord showed me a picture of ...." "When I was praying for you, the Lord kept bringing a scripture to my mind." "I sense the Lord saying..." or "I saw a vision of..." Prophetic intercessors really can be used by the Lord to speak an encouraging word that edifies and lifts up someone in the Body of Christ. However, let me repeat that all the parts of the body are needed to make up the whole, with each joint supplying what others need. One type of intercessory calling and expression is not better than another. The key in intercessory prayer is to know how we are called and then be good stewards of what the Lord has entrusted to us.

"From him the whole body, joined and held together by every supporting ligament, grows and builds itself up in love, as each part does its work." Ephesians 4:16 (NIV)

As you can see, there are many ministry expressions within the Body of Christ where a prophetic intercessor can be effective. As with any intercessor, it is important to identify your personal prayer burden as part of the process of finding your place in ministry. If you are not sure, begin to journal the kinds of things that motivate you to pray and look for a pattern. If you find that you pray a lot for missionaries, you could have a heart to either be a personal intercessor, like an armor bearer, or one who prays for nations, or both. The pattern you discover is a good indicator of what your intercessory burden is. The next step is to ask the Lord to show you how this type of prayer burden can best be expressed in the Body of Christ either on a prayer team or in serving in another ministry in the local church.

In Conclusion

In this chapter, we have defined prophetic intercession and defined how the revelation gifts function. I have also attempted to broaden your view of how a prophetic intercessor can be a tremendous asset in other areas of ministry in the local church. Although prayer may be a primary focus for a prophetic intercessor, it may be only one aspect of how they have been called. Over the years, I have discovered that prophetic intercessors, as well as other prayer warriors, are some of the strongest ministers in the local church. In addition to their intercessory call, many have a burning passion to be part of the hands-on aspect of ministry. Rarely are prophetic intercessors content to just be involved in prayer. They usually seek out other ministry outlets, such as ministering to children, youth, or young adults. They may minister in music, at the altar, in compassion outreaches, in counseling, on a deliverance team, or by leading a home fellowship. Most prophetic intercessors love to minister to people and have such a heart to serve! For this reason, it is important that church leadership does not think that the only thing intercessors do is pray. For most intercessors, prayer is only one aspect of how they have been called.

Chapter 2

Ellen Laitinen

The Prophetic Prayer Flow

"Now He who searches the hearts knows what the mind of the spirit is, because He makes intercession for the saints according to the will of God."   Romans 8:27

As we have previously discussed, one of the distinctive qualities of prophetic intercessors is in their prayer flow. Because the revelation gifts operate as part of their unique expression, prophetic intercessors enter into prayer times very differently from other praying people. One major difference is that they remain on the same prayer focus and wait to hear from the Lord about how to pray for a particular person or situation. When prophetic intercessors are part of a prayer team, there are some important guidelines to remember. Prophetic protocol is an important principle because it has to do with how the members of the Body of Christ should flow in harmony with one another and maintain the integrity of the team.

To gain a clearer understanding of how this protocol works we will discuss these guidelines in the context of a prophetic intercessory team (ten to twelve people) with an ongoing prayer assignment to pray protection over the church vision.

In this prayer assignment we will ask the Lord to reveal three things as we stand watch and pray. All involve a prophetic activation in discerning: 1) the direction of the Holy Spirit and what God desires to accomplish; 2) the schemes of the enemy that oppose or hinder God's purposes; 3) the Lord's wisdom about how to counter any spiritual opposition.

I have found the following prayer guidelines to be very helpful, not only in activating prophetic prayer, but also in reflecting how believers need to honor and respect each other in the process. Please understand that these guidelines are not intended to be unchangeable rules, but tools for training intercessors in what encourages prophetic prayer in a group setting. Much grace and understanding needs to be extended to intercessors who are new to this kind of prayer or young in their prophetic expression. My objective as a prayer leader is to create a safe atmosphere where intercessors can learn and blossom in their prophetic gifts. This atmosphere includes establishing a clear sense of order to the meetings by setting some basic guidelines that everyone can follow.

Prophetic Prayer Guidelines

1. Come with your heart prepared to pray.

Preparation is such an important part of intercession. Intercession is an important time to lay our own agendas aside, cast our cares onto the Lord, sensitize our spirits to hear the voice of the Lord and pray the things that are on the Father's heart. We will cover this area of how to spiritually prepare our hearts to intercede in a later chapter.

2. Our assignment is to pray in accordance with the vision and calling of our local church, not make up our own direction. So we will watch for what the Lord is currently doing or desires to do as well as for any spiritual opposition that hinders the church from moving forward.

It is very important to be aware of the vision and direction of the senior pastor. As we come into agreement with the vision of the church leadership, the Lord will give us insight to pray protection and even to discern how the enemy can try to oppose the forward movement of this vision. Praying in agreement with a vision is based on the understanding that God has given the leaders His vision of what He wants to accomplish through the local church in advancing the kingdom.

This is why I always pay close attention to the prophetic words given corporately, the sermon, and the vision articulated to the church. Along with the discernment God has given me as a watchman, these guidelines enable me to keep watch in praying protection over the prophetic direction of the church. Intercessors do not set the direction of the church, but pray protection over it.

When a watchman is keeping watch, many times prophetic insight will come in the form of a strategy that will help the church keep moving forward on the right course. For example, the Lord may reveal that for a breakthrough, the church may need to fast and pray, enter into a time of repentance, or host a special time for corporate worship. Often God will reveal through a prophetic word how to specifically target our prayers. These types of prophetic insight need to be submitted to the senior pastor, especially when the insight involves the congregation, and used at the leadership's discretion. Although it may appear that the intercessor is giving a kind of direction, actually the revelation comes as a result of the vision already set in motion by the church leadership. As long as the intercessors stay in alignment with the leadership, this prophetic insight can serve as an armor of protection, wisdom about how to mobilize the church for prayer, or a simple confirmation of the prophetic direction.

3. Be sensitive to one another as we pray. Remember that this is a team and more importantly the Body of Christ. So we need to prefer one another and appreciate the different gifts of the people on the team. If someone is speaking, be careful to not talk over them or interrupt. The KEY to our effectiveness in prayer has to do with our ability to pray in unity.

We need to remember that prayer is not a competition to see who can articulate the most prophetic insight or have the most powerful prayer. It is so important for our actions and attitudes to not grieve the Holy Spirit. Instead, we need to reflect the proper respect of the other members of the body. At times, it means you need to step aside and allow someone else to speak.

In our unique gifts, all of us have an important part to play. Each person on the team needs to feel the freedom to express the gift God has put within them. When we prefer and defer to one another, it helps to create an atmosphere of safety, especially for the more quiet people to be willing to risk participating. Our intercession is not nearly as effective when we talk over someone, interrupt, or are impatient. Furthermore, this grieves the Holy Spirit. Whenever I have seen a lack of respect, I have noticed also an atmosphere change in the room. Typically what was a safe environment is now infiltrated with a spirit of contention and strife. Along with contention usually come some demonic associates, such as frustration, anger, chaos, and confusion. Disrespect provides a welcome mat that opens the door for these kinds of evil spirits. This kind of atmosphere never should be found in an intercessory prayer meeting. It is not only out of order, but is also unbecoming for people called to partner with the Lord.

4. Whoever is leading the team should set the prayer point. The team then prays for this focus until the next prayer point is set by the team leader.

Setting the prayer focus is important to activating the prophetic prayer flow. Leading out in a prayer point is very much like being the first one to prophesy corporately. The first one to pray is initiating the prophetic theme for the revelation that follows.

The Word of God says that prophecy is subject to the prophet[33]. This means that if you are following someone who is prophesying a word and the prophetic word God has given you does not follow in theme with what has already been said, then you need to wait to release your prophecy at a more appropriate moment. This same protocol applies to both corporate prophecy and to prophetic intercession.

During a meeting, we may only pray for a couple of prayer points, but the time given to pray over a certain point is what activates the prophetic gifts. Although the initial prayers may not seem too prophetic, as we continue in prayer and listen to hear the voice of the Lord, we allow the Holy Spirit an opportunity to reveal things to us through the prophetic gifts. When the revelation gifts are active, there is usually a prophetic prayer flow that follows. During the prophetic prayer flow, more of the team receives insight and knows how to pray more specifically. The prophetic flow is very much like putting a jigsaw puzzle together. As each one brings forth their insight, the picture forming becomes more complete. This insight shows us how to pray more targeted prayers. I call this pattern of prayer prophetic building. Prophetic building creates a depth and perception about what God is revealing. Imagine an object positioned in the center of a room. If a group of people stand in different spots around the object, each person views it from a slightly different angle. These varying perspectives give us

---

[33] 1 Corinthians 14:32

depth and perception. It is the difference between viewing an object from the perspective of a flat plane—one dimensional— and seeing it multi-dimensionally. In a similar way, prophetic building allows prophetic intercessors to have a fuller understanding of what God is revealing about a person or situation. As prophetic intercessors learn to pray together, the mix of revelation gifts creates a synergy that increases the ability of the intercessors to discern the wisdom of God and pray more targeted prayers.

Accurately discerning the Lord's direction for prayer also helps to activate the prophetic gifts within the intercessory team. God desires to partner with us in prayer. In His wisdom He has created the universe so that when we pray, he moves on behalf of those prayers[34]. When we take the time to discern God's heart and pray His will in a situation, we will see Him move mightily in accomplishing His kingdom purposes. The Lord is so delighted when we are willing vessels for the Holy Spirit to move through[35].

6. Avoid praying for multiple subjects all at once. Take time to hear the Lord and pray through each prayer point.

When we pray for multiple subjects all at once, it short circuits the rest of the team from hearing and participating in what could turn into a prophetic prayer flow. I encourage the intercessors to be short and to the point so others have an

---

[34] Psalm 34:17
[35] Ezekiel 22:30

opportunity to express the piece that the Lord is revealing to them. This takes self-control, especially for prophetic intercessors! Prophetic intercessors often start with a prophetic sense about a particular prayer focus and then discern other things that tempt them to jump ahead in the set prayer focus.

When praying on a team, it is an important discipline not to continue to pray beyond the initial revelation that the Lord is prompting unless it is clear that additional revelation relates to the prayer topic. I usually tell the intercessors if their prayer goes long, be sure that there is a clear leading of the Holy Spirit and stay on topic. One reason for limiting the length of prayers has to do with team dynamics. It is frustrating to listen to someone pray for a long period of time, especially if they have gotten sidetracked. Prophetic intercessors can usually discern when the anointing for a prayer has ended. When there is a strong prophetic flow within a team, there is also a confirmation in the spirit for the rest of the team as each intercessor prays. When someone is praying by the leading of the Holy Spirit, it is easy to remain engaged and follow along in agreement. When someone gets sidetracked, the rest of team is aware of it.

7. Usually when the Lord releases us from a prayer focus, we will all sense it and there may be a long silence. When that occurs, the team leader may lead out in another prayer point or continue to wait in God's presence.

A period of silence is not always how we move from prayer point to prayer point, but it can be an indicator. The Lord usually will prompt the team leader when to close the prayer focus and move on. Sometimes this change of direction is preceded by a silence. Learn to be comfortable with these quiet moments. Do not allow an initial uneasiness with what appears to be a long silence prompt you to pray. During moments of silence, we may receive further revelation. At the end of a prayer focus, we also may experience a strong presence of the Lord. Times of silence are when the Holy Spirit ministers a sense of peace and joy to our spirit as we wait quietly in His presence. It is important to not be too quick to fill in the times of silence during prayer.

8. Do not use prayer to preach sermons. We are meant to pray what is on God's heart.

When you pray, be sensitive to the Holy Spirit and be careful not to use prayer to preach a sermon. Although the message may be great, it has the potential to take the listeners off the prayer focus. It is certainly okay to use a passage in scripture as the backdrop for your prayers. Often I find myself clarifying a scriptural principle in how God is leading us to pray or as a biblical reference point.

9. If you receive a vision, a scripture, or a prophetic word, feel free to share it while the team is focused on that prayer point.

Many times, when people are receiving a prophetic word, they are afraid to share it because they are afraid to be incorrect, the meaning is not clear, or they do not see how it fits in the current prayer flow. If fear is the only thing holding you back from sharing what you sense prophetically, then please understand that your revelation gift should be viewed from a stewardship standpoint[36]. When the Lord entrusts us with something, including a prophetic gift, we need to be good stewards of what He has given to us. It is more important to be faithful with what God has entrusted to you than resist sharing it because of fear.

If you are sincerely feeling prompted by the Holy Spirit to bring forth a prophetic word or impression, then your responsibility is to be faithful to submit what God has given you to your prayer leader or pastor. As you walk in obedience, God then shoulders the burden of confirming the word! Remember, if the prophetic insight is from the Lord, it is *His* word and He is watching over that word to perform it!

"The word of the Lord came to me: 'What do you see, Jeremiah?'" 'I see the branch of an almond tree,'" I replied."

The Lord said to me, 'You have seen correctly, for I am watching to see that my word is fulfilled.'

Jeremiah 1:11-12 (NIV)

It is interesting to see the progression here in Jeremiah. First, the Lord stirs up the prophetic gift in Jeremiah by asking him what he sees. When Jeremiah looks, he sees the branch of an almond tree[37]. Jeremiah then tells the Lord what he sees. This

---

[36] Reference Chapter 4
[37] A vision

is very much how the prophetic gift works. God shows us something and then we speak forth what he reveals.

It is important to note that, after Jeremiah articulates what he sees, God confirms to Jeremiah two things: 1) Jeremiah has seen correctly and 2) God is watching over that word to fulfill it! So as Jeremiah was faithful with what the Lord had revealed to him (in this case by speaking it forth), God in turn was faithful to bring the confirmation! It is clear from this passage that God cares deeply about the fulfillment of His word and even takes an active role in watching over it to see it fulfilled!

What a wonderful representation of how the prophetic gift is intended to flow between God and man! There is always a purposing and a creative power contained within a prophetic word to accomplish all that God intends. Likewise, this is also a picture of how prophetic intercession operates. When the revelation gifts are in operation, we begin to see and then declare what we discern to be the will or direction of God in how we pray. This forms an agreement between God and man. It is this agreement that brings about the establishing of God's Word in the earth[38].

10. If you receive a vision or impression that is not clear, WAIT on the Lord until it is clear and then share it. If the team has moved onto another prayer focus, wait until there is an appropriate moment to share during the meeting, at the end, or

---

[38] Isaiah 55:11

with the leader privately afterwards. Remember you can always pray a prophetic word, sense, or impression through on your own.

Many intercessors experience a prophetic impression or vision that is not clear enough for them to feel prompted to share during a meeting. Here are a few reasons it may not be clear: 1) God has not finished giving you the revelation; 2) the meaning and how it fits may become clear later in the meeting because of other revelation shared by another team member. Remember, not everything God reveals to you is to be shared. The Lord may require you to pray some things through on your own.

Another key in moving in the prophetic gifts is discerning if the Lord is prompting you to speak or remain silent. Intercessors who are just learning to move in the prophetic gifts often think it is urgent to share everything that the Lord speaks to them. This is where a mentor is helpful in guiding the intercessor to understand what the Lord is requiring of them and to not be so impulsive in their sharing.

11. Keep the confidentiality of prayer points when it is of a personal nature.

At times prayer points are of a sensitive or personal nature. These prayer points may come from within the team about a personal need or from the pastoral staff. The basic rule of prayer teams is to maintain confidentiality in the things entrusted to us that are of a private nature. They should not be discussed *outside* the prayer team[39].

12. If you receive a prophetic word during the week that has to do with something that has been prayed about, please e-mail or call the team leader.

Many times after a prayer meeting, an intercessor will receive further clarification about something the team has prayed about or discernment of what is currently happening in the spiritual realm that may need prayer. This prophetic insight should be given to the prayer leader to determine whether to mobilize the rest of the team or alert the pastor. It is really helpful to have a prayer pastor or prayer coordinator to whom intercessors can go to in discerning whether something is urgent. Intercessors also need to be sensitive about not overwhelming their pastor with all the "revelation" they are receiving. If there is not a head intercessor to mentor this process, then church leadership should encourage intercessors to wait for the Lord to prompt them before sharing a prophetic word.

Not all prophetic words are to be shared. Ask the Lord what he wants you to do. Some things the Lord has prompted me to do in response to prophetic revelation: 1) pray it through myself; 2) submit it to leadership; 3) wait until there is a release in my spirit to share it. Generally, people will experience an inner peace and a prompting of the Holy Spirit when it is time to

---

[39] Reference Chapter 9

release a prophetic word. However, you may indeed feel your heart pounding!

Waiting for this prompting of the Holy Spirit is especially important when you understand how the Lord has a special timing for everything. You may ask, "Why would the Lord give me a prophetic word if it was not time to share it?" Sometimes the Lord will alert you so that you can be in prayer for the release of that word. I have seen many things prophetically and held them in my heart for long periods of time. Sometimes the Lord wanted me to pray about revelation first and then at a future date release it prophetically.

Intercessors need to be careful not to allow their spiritual identity to be determined by their prophetic gifting. Some intercessors fall into the trap of thinking the more revelation they receive and share, the more spiritual they are. Exercising self-control in releasing a word is difficult when there is a constant need to prove yourself. Remember, your identity is in Christ not in how "prophetic" you are. Spiritual gifts were designed to be an extension of God's love and mercy in the earth. They were intended to reveal more about God's identity than our own. We need to remember that we are His vessels in conveying prophetic revelations.

13. Some of the things we will discern may need to be submitted to the church leadership. Please remember that once we do submit something prophetically, it is extremely important to leave it alone. Our job as intercessors or watchmen is to submit what we sense the Lord is speaking to us prophetically and then trust our leadership to seek the Lord about it.

This point is extremely important for intercessors to understand. It is not our job to *prove* what we have discerned prophetically is correct or to *demand* that it be acted upon. Our job is to be good stewards of what we believe the Lord is saying and humbly submit this to our leadership. Submitting prophetic revelation to spiritual authority is vital for the proper communication and trust to emerge between pastors and intercessors. It is also foundational for the right kind of prayer support to be in place to support the work of the ministry. Senior pastors need the freedom to seek the Lord and administrate prophetic words according to what the Lord is revealing to them. Pastors are responsible before God in how they lead their congregation. This is why in Hebrews 13, exhorts us:

"Obey your spiritual leaders and do what they say. Their work is to watch over your souls, and they know they are accountable to God. Give them reason to do this joyfully and not with sorrow. That would certainly not be for your benefit."

Hebrews 13:17a (NLT)

You might say, "But you do not understand, my pastor is not even prophetic." Yes but, prophetic or not, your pastor can still hear from God. God will move on your behalf if you will stay properly submitted to the God-given authority in your life[40].

What about the pastor who seems to avoid intercessors or does not seem to understand them? Before you start judging, please understand that some pastors have had horrible experiences with intercessors and have no idea if their experience with you will be any different. Some trust may need to be rebuilt. This is a real opportunity for an intercessor to show God's love and compassion by looking for opportunities to bless and serve their pastor in addition to keeping them in prayer. As you continue to honor your leader in this way, you will be amazed at the miracles God will do in blessing your relationship with your pastor[41].

14. At the end of our prayer time, please do not pray after the person who is designated to close out the prayer time.

As a point of order, closing the prayer time properly is very important. Many times, and quite innocently I might add, intercessors get additional revelation that they want to pray after the closing prayer. They usually feel quite urgent about their revelation and insist upon sharing it. This is where intercessors need to trust the Lord and stay submitted to those responsible to closing out the prayer time.

---

[40] Reference Chapter 7
[41] reference chapters 5 and 6

Ellen Laitinen

When prayer is extended beyond the closing, it usurps the leader's authority in discerning the time to close. I have seen prayer meetings get out of order quickly when someone prays beyond the designated closing. Usurping of authority opens the door for a spirit of chaos, confusion, manipulation, control, and even witchcraft to enter into a meeting.

So what do you do if you get a prophetic word that you sense needs to be shared? Hold onto it and either pray it through yourself or share it with the leader afterwards. Asking the leader for permission to share it puts that leader in an awkward position to refuse. As I have mentioned before, not everything that you receive needs to be shared. If giving a prophetic word does not fit with the stated order of the established authority, then wait to share it. God has designed prophecy to be subject to the direction of the prophet, which means we can exercise self-control in releasing a word in an orderly fashion.

"Remember that people who prophesy are in control of their spirit and can wait their turn. For God is not a God of disorder but of peace, as in all the other churches."

I Corinthians 14:32-33 (NLT)

Prophetic Confirmation

When you are just beginning to pray prophetically on a team, what are some indicators that what you're sensing is correct? When the Lord really wants to communicate something important, He is faithful to bring confirmations from various sources:

- There will be a peace and a witness in your spirit

- Others may have received a similar word or impression

- There may be a witness in the spirit from others on the team

- Many times the Lord will give a scripture to confirm a prophecy or prophetic impression

- There may be a historical or current validation of facts

- A confirmation from the church leadership when a word is submitted

Prayer Strategies

Many times in the course of the prayer meeting, the Lord will reveal a strategy of how to pray. An example of a prayer strategy would be in performing a prophetic act--an action done in the natural that symbolizes God's will on earth as it is established in heaven. It also serves as a type of agreement that announces to the demonic realm that they have been defeated and through this act you are serving an eviction notice. As we have discussed, God's Word carries with it a supernatural and creative ability to push back the powers of darkness, in order to make a place for the fulfillment of His word. So, when God speaks, the enemy has no more power to resist. This is how we gain spiritual ground. Needless to say, agreement with God's Word and His will is a powerful tool in defeating the schemes of the enemy.

The Lord may also prompt us to wage war with a prophetic word. As you pray, you remind and thank God for what He has promised, through a Rhema Word, a biblical promise, or a prophecy[42], until God brings the fulfillment.

General Guidelines for Small or Large Groups

When intercessors are praying in a large group or small group setting, I ask them to keep a few courtesies in mind. The first thing is to be conscious of how to enter a room where the prayer meeting is being held. It amazes me how often people enter a prayer meeting while in the middle of a conversation with someone else. A loud conversation can be very disruptive to a group that is either quietly praying or to the leader who is facilitating the prayer time. If a conversation is not related to prayer and is important, then it is best to go into another room or location. I also ask people, when they enter either a large or small group prayer setting, to be sensitive to how the Holy Spirit is moving in the room and join in the flow. For example, if people are worshiping, enter in to the room in a spirit of worship. If people are praying aloud or in their prayer language, join in the flow gracefully. A good guideline is to not pray louder than the volume in the room.

---

[42] Isaiah 62:6-7

What about praying for someone in a corporate prayer setting? In our church we have around 150 people attend our weekly prayer meeting. The first portion of prayer time is unstructured, so people are free to walk around and pray. In this kind of a setting it would be appropriate to quietly pray for someone, as long as the prayer does not distract someone who is trying to pray nearby. We try to avoid starting conversations that are not related to prayer or are distracting to others.

Also make sure that all pagers or cell phones are either turned off or are on vibrate. There is nothing more distracting than a cell phone going off in the middle of a prayer meeting.

Another guideline is to leave your personal prayer agenda at the door unless the structure of the prayer meeting includes an unstructured time to pray on your own. When you attend a prayer meeting, it is important to stay in the flow of that meeting. For example, if the prayer time is designated to pray for a particular issue, avoid praying for unrelated topics.

In small group settings it's important to listen to what being prayed. Sometimes intercessors get so focused on what they want to pray that they don't pay attention to what *is* being prayed; listening is an important aspect of remaining in the flow of how the Holy Spirit is prompting others to pray. Also, it is not good to talk over people, but to wait patiently until the person is finished praying aloud before beginning another prayer.

   Ellen Laitinen

These suggestions may seem obvious, but after participating in hundreds of prayer meetings over the past twenty years, I can tell you truly that these basic principles are not commonly understood. Is this a complete list? No, I am sure there are other courtesies. However, we are covering a broad spectrum and each situation may require different guidelines.

In Conclusion

In this chapter, we have reviewed some basic guidelines that help in the activation of this prophetic flow as well as some general prayer guidelines for participating in small and large group settings. Prophetic intercession can be of such great value to the church, especially in praying protection over the advancement of a regional or local church vision. It is the hearing and seer aspect of the revelation gifts that enables the prophetic intercessor to pray with a type of precision that not only agrees with God's direction in this advance, but it also reflects the Father's heart when we choose to honor one another in the process.

Chapter 3

Mentoring the Prophetic Intercessor Part I

"But God demonstrates His own love toward us, in that while we were still sinners, Christ died for us."   Romans 5:8

When it becomes clear that one has a prophetic gift as part of her or his prayer expression, how is this prophetic intercessor to be mentored? The mentoring process begins by first understanding the importance of intercession from God's perspective. This perspective will be the major emphasis for this chapter as we discuss the biblical values necessary in shaping the heart of a prophetic intercessor. We will cover both broad and specific areas, such as distinguishing the prophetic gifts, understanding God's perspective of intercession, preparing one's heart to intercede, practicing proper stewardship, setting right priorities, and recognizing the seasons of spiritual growth. I would like to offer these as the biblical perspectives necessary in the initial mentoring of a prophetic intercessor.

Distinguishing the Prophetic Gifts

Many intercessors in the initial stage of discovering their prophetic gift are still trying to identify which prophetic gift is in operation as they pray and how their particular gift functions. It may be confusing if the person has more than one prophetic gift, so one of the first steps is assisting intercessors in this process of identification.

When an intercessor experiences a dream, vision, prophetic sensing, or a Rhema Word, it is helpful to identify from which revelation gift the prophetic expression is operating. We have already established that each of the prophetic expressions will flow from one of the four prophetic gifts. For example, the revelation contained within a prophecy, vision, dream, sensing, or Rhema Word could be a word of wisdom, a word of knowledge, the discernment of spirits, or prophecy. With people who are in this early stage, I try to say things like the following:

- "That vision you had was a word of knowledge because it revealed knowledge you did not know."

- "That dream you told me about was some clear discernment about what demonic spirit is in operation."

- "That Rhema Word is giving us some wisdom as to what direction we need to pray."

- "That prophetic sense you had of a strong anointing of healing is revealing wisdom in how God is about to prophetically move in the meeting."

These kinds of statements are very helpful for an intercessor to begin to identify her or his particular prophetic gift.

Physical Manifestations

In the area of discernment of spirits, some intercessors, especially those with this gift, may experience a physical manifestation as a form of discernment. Personally, when I discern emotional pain in someone's life, my hand will start to ache. Many years ago I was attending a home fellowship meeting where the leaders began to gather around a man to pray. This man was visiting our group, so I was unfamiliar with his background. In fact when he asked for prayer, I had not initially heard why he needed prayer. I stood about ten feet away and extended my hand in his direction as others gathered around him to pray. I noticed that my hand began to ache as it was extended in his direction. In fact, it hurt so much that I had to put my arm down. Amazingly, the pain instantly disappeared. I thought this was very strange, so I extended my arm again and once more began to feel an ache. I discovered each time I raised my hand in this man's direction I felt physical pain. When I would lower my arm, the pain would stop.

Suddenly I remembered a similar time, several years before, when I had laid hands on someone to pray and had felt pain in my hand. At that time, I discerned the person was experiencing significant emotional pain. I felt impressed to pray about God healing emotional pain. When I prayed, the ache disappeared. So I wondered if this was the reason that I was experiencing pain in my hand again. Was the Lord giving me some discernment? As I pondered this question, I felt the Holy Spirit prompt me to pray about emotional pain again. I explained to the home fellowship leaders what I was sensing and asked if I could pray for the man. They agreed. Two things happened when I prayed: the man felt the Lord ministering to him and my hand stopped hurting.

Physical manifestations can be a form of discernment. I have known intercessors who experience severe headaches when they discern oppression. They feel tightness around their forehead that they often describe as the feeling of a band around their head when they discern witchcraft or a strong occult presence. Others have discovered that the back of their neck feels stiff when they discern witchcraft. At times, I have felt unnatural waves of tiredness that alerted me there was strong spiritual opposition present.

Most of what an intercessor experiences during prayer is a form of prophetic revelation. When an intercessor is experiencing discernment through physical symptoms, there are a few things to keep in mind. First, with this kind of discernment, any physical symptoms should disappear when the Lord reveals how to pray and the prayer burden begins to lift. What if the symptoms do not disappear? Three things should be considered:

- Is there any natural cause that could explain the physical manifestation you are experiencing (lack of sleep, recent injury or illness)? The symptom may not be discernment.

- Have you prayed through any prayer burden associated with this physical manifestation? Many times these symptoms disappear after your burden to pray lifts.

- If you sense there is a spiritual aspect to what you are experiencing physically and the Lord is not revealing a direction of how to pray, then rebuke the symptom. The symptom may be a spiritual attack.

Let me be clear that not every ache and pain is spiritual discernment, but the intercessors with the gift of discernment of spirits do have a heightened awareness of the spiritual climate in the atmosphere around them. As previously mentioned, this awareness often involves a "feeling" aspect relating to the physical senses, particularly in an ability to see, hear, smell, and touch.

An Ability to See into the Spiritual Realm

Some intercessors have had experiences of seeing into the spiritual realm through dreams, visions, or an open vision. Others have even seen angels, demons, or some form of spiritual activity[43].

Personally, I have experienced many prophetic dreams and visions that either communicated a message from God or revealed spiritual activity as a form of discernment.

---

[43] Reference Chapter 2

Hearing – Another Physical Sense

Hearing is another physical sense that can be heightened to hear the voice of the Lord, angels, or the voice of the accuser. Some people have even heard the audible voice of God, although I have found this is a very rare occurrence.

Once I attended a conference on worship in New Hampshire. The presence of God was so strong during worship that, even from the back row, I could barely remain standing. I found myself compelled to utter "Holy, Holy, Holy" during the worship. I have never experienced the presence of God as powerfully before or since that day. After the last worship session of the conference, I began to hear a sound of what I could only surmise as angels singing. For several hours afterwards, as I drove from New Hampshire to Vermont, I heard this unusual sound. It was as if someone was broadcasting supernatural music in my ears. Others around me did not seem to hear the music. The melodious sound I heard is very difficult to put into words. It is best described as a combination of music and the roar of many voices singing in harmony. The only thing to which I can compare it is the sound of a crowd of several thousand talking all at once. I could not distinguish any words, yet there seemed to be some musical blend of harmonies and rhythm. I remember thinking to myself that I was listening to the music of heaven.

Ellen Laitinen

The Heart of an Intercessor

At the core of every intercessor should be God's heart for redemption. This is a vital perspective to embrace as it serves to help safeguard us from becoming critical or judgmental in our thoughts and actions toward one another.

Romans 5:8 underscores the depth to which the Father and His Son Jesus were willing to go for the redemption of mankind by declaring that Jesus died for us while we were yet sinners with all of our imperfections, sins, and wrong attitudes. Based on the forgiveness God granted us and the price that was paid to secure it, we are left without excuse in extending the same love and forgiveness toward others.

As intercessors, it is vital to keep this perspective. The minute we become critical or judgmental, we lose our ability to effectively intercede in a way that reflects God's heart. Unfortunately, the enemy especially attacks intercessors in the soul realm through offenses, misunderstandings, and unjust circumstances. The minute we respond in anger and allow ourselves to become frustrated, we lose God's perspective of the situation. How is this true? In our wrong response we stop placing our confidence in God. Instead we rely on our own understanding of people and circumstances.

If you are faced with a situation where someone has wronged you and you have tried to confront the person in love without success, understand that God has called you to a place of prayer concerning the person or situation. With this call, there can be a tremendous battle in your soul. However a wrong response can cause you to become ineffective as an intercessor because you have not recognized the true nature of this battle nor your position in it.

There is an expression, "Hurting people hurt people"; it is very true. Hurtful people need our prayers rather than our judgment of them, which is hard when we have suffered from their attitudes and actions. It is particularly difficult when the target of an offense is in an area where you are very sensitive. That is when it is the most challenging to have a right response. As an intercessor, however, it is crucial to press through your own sense of pain by submitting any sense of injustice or wrongdoing to God and trusting Him for the results. Sounds easy? It is not. In fact having the right attitude can be heart-wrenching. But reaching deeper into your faith to trust God when you are tempted to be offended is absolutely essential to resisting the devil and disrupting his tactics to bring about division or further offense.

"Therefore submit to God. Resist the devil and he will flee from you." James 4:7

Many times when someone has a lot of emotional pain in their life, it causes blindness to the way he or she is treating others. Sometimes a person's blindness is the reason why the process of confrontation does not work. Until God begins to heal people, they often cannot see how their actions have impacted others. This is why it is important to remain in a posture of prayer for them. God's heart for hurting people is always for restoration and healing in the areas they have experienced pain, trauma or injustices.

One question we should always consider: Are my actions towards a hurtful person restorative or adding more condemnation? This is a difficult question, but one that we must ask of ourselves if we are going to maintain a posture of intercession. Believe me, I know this battle all too well. I have my own share of bumps and bruises from the times I have not responded in a way that reflected God's redemptive heart toward others. Not only does a soulish response make things worse, but now God has to discipline you.

"But even if you suffer for doing what is right, God will reward you for it. So don't be afraid and don't worry. Instead, you must worship Christ as Lord of your life. And if you are asked about your Christian hope, always be ready to explain it. But you must do this in a gentle and respectful way. Keep your conscience clear. Then if people speak evil against you, they will be ashamed when they see what a good life you live because you belong to Christ. Remember it is better to suffer for doing good, if that is what God wants, than to suffer for doing wrong."   *1 Peter 3:14-17 (NLT)*

The scripture is very clear about the perspective we are to embrace when we suffer unjustly:

- Remember that God will reward you for it.

- Worship God in the midst of suffering and trust He is in control of the circumstances.

- Do not allow your difficult circumstances to interfere with a readiness to share your Christian faith in a gentle and respectful way.

- Guard your actions so that you might maintain a clear conscience.

- Maintain a position of godliness so those who would speak evil about you will be ashamed when they see the Christian integrity in which you live.

- If you experience suffering, let it be for doing good rather than for doing wrong.

The truth is we are ultimately accountable to God for all our actions and we need to keep that foremost in our mind when we encounter various trials. The promise is that we can find comfort in how God will reward us for what we have suffered or endured. So the real question is, "Can we trust God in the midst of our difficulty and remain confident in how He is working all things out for our good?"[44]

---

[44] Romans 8:28

 Ellen Laitinen

As intercessors, we must remember that God has a greater redemptive purpose at work in our lives through the difficulties we face. Our trials are not just about us. God's greater purpose is at work with what He wants to accomplish in and through us. God wants to bring restoration and healing to our lives, our families, our neighborhoods, our places of work, and our city. As mentioned, it is important that we begin to see the relational difficulties and injustices we experience as a call to prayer. Responding to each of life's adversities as a call to prayer is vital to overcoming the powers of darkness and seeing the kingdom of God advance not only in our personal sphere of influence, but also in our city and nation.

Standing in the Gap

"So I sought for a man among them who would make a wall, and stand in the gap before Me on behalf of the land, that I should not destroy it; but I found no one." *Ezekiel 22:30*

The gap in this passage refers to a breach or an opening in what once was a fortified wall. Walls are symbolic of boundaries and protection much like the walls of ancient cities. When there is a breach in the wall, this opening makes the city vulnerable to attack by an invading army. This principle is true in the lives of individuals, families, cities, or nations. Wherever moral integrity and godly standards are not maintained, there is a spiritual breach making that person, family, city, or nation susceptible to demonic attacks.

In this verse in Ezekiel there has already been a moral decay and God is about to bring judgment upon the land. Because of His redemptive nature, God searches for one person who is willing to stand in the gap and pray that God would not destroy the city. What's really happening here? God is looking for someone to stand in the place where the breach has occurred and also make a wall. What kind of wall is the Lord referring to? From God's perspective, each person who is willing to stand in the gap becomes a living stone that, together with others, makes up a wall of protection while God's redeeming work is bringing about a restoration.

The act of standing in the gap in prayer is parallel to Jesus in His role as the great intercessor. Hebrews 7:25 declares, *"He (Jesus) always lives to make intercession for them."* When we pray, we add our faith and agreement to the advance of God's kingdom. This advance comes from Christ's primary intercessory focus which is for mankind to receive salvation.

Many Christians have received salvation through Christ, but this is only part of God's redemptive work. God's redemptive plan also includes mental, emotional, and physical healing. We are all at different stages of healing and deliverance, so we need to be very careful to extend grace and forgiveness toward people who have areas in their lives that still need healing. In our relationships we encounter conflicts because people are at various stages of healing and because of demonic opposition. Therefore, in spite of difficult personal challenges, we cannot let ourselves be derailed by relational conflicts or offenses. As intercessors, we need to submit to God's process of dealing with us and His timing in our trials and conflicts and remain in the place of prayer.

Heart Preparation

The process of the Lord preparing our heart for the service of intercession is a necessary act of humility that we must embrace. The role of an intercessor reflects the very heart of Jesus himself to intercede as he hung on a cross between heaven and earth to bring about our redemption. If we are going to emulate this same purity of heart in our intercession for others, we must also allow our hearts to be tested and cleansed.

An interesting perspective of this kind of inner working is depicted in John 14. Jesus begins to prepare the disciples for his impending betrayal and death. In verse 30, Jesus makes an interesting statement to his disciples of His spiritual condition and the resulting authority He has over the evil one.

"I will no longer talk much with you, for the ruler of this world is coming, and he has nothing in Me."   *John 14:30*

In this verse Jesus knows that his time on earth is coming to a close and the ruler of this world is coming to work his own plans. Jesus wants his disciples to know that, regardless of the apparent triumph of evil they will see soon, things are not what they seem. Jesus knew through the circumstances of His death and crucifixion it would appear that Satan has won a great victory. Jesus is telling His disciples that, although the evil one is approaching, Satan has no power over Him. How could Jesus make such a statement? We need to remember that Jesus, who was both fully God and fully human, had lived a sinless life.

"For we do not have a High Priest who cannot sympathize with our weaknesses, but was in all points tempted as we are, yet without sin."   *Hebrews 4:15*

In His human form, Jesus also submitted to the dealings of God. We see this also in the book of Mark. After Jesus was baptized by John the Baptist and the Father declared that Jesus is His beloved Son, the word says:

"Immediately the Spirit drove Him into the wilderness. And He was tempted by Satan, and was with wild beasts; and the angels ministered to Him."   *Mark 1:13*

The temptations Jesus experienced were in preparation for his earthly ministry. The depth to which He was tempted and overcame the evil one in the wilderness also gave Him the authority to defeat this enemy at the cross. That is why Jesus could say with confidence in John 14:30, *"He (Satan) has nothing in me."* In other words, Satan could not find a foothold within Jesus to exercise his power. Because the power of sin was broken at the cross, Jesus offers us this same advantage if we will submit to God's dealings with our sins and our iniquitous patterns.

Take time to Examine

When I am training intercessors, I often challenge them to take a period of time, a couple of weeks or a month, to ask the Lord to reveal anything in their lives that could hinder them in their ministry of intercession. I challenge them to seek the Lord about places in their lives where there may be anger, pride, unforgiveness, control, manipulation, fear, unbelief, greed, selfish ambition, relational conflicts, offenses, and so on. These sins are the enemies of the soul that can usher in a worldly, fleshly, or demonic influence.

We need to particularly watch our thoughts because they are the gateway to our mind, will, and emotions. Any thought that is left unchecked carries the potential to produce a resulting attitude or action. Our thinking has three sources: thoughts inspired by the Holy Spirit, demonic thoughts, and our own human reasoning. Just having an ungodly thought is not sinful. However, when we begin to dwell on an ungodly thought, it becomes dangerous. Dwelling on an ungodly thought could tempt us to form an agreement with it. When we agree with an ungodly thought, it plants itself as a seed in our heart. Then it takes root as a belief system that can influence our perception of life or worldview. This is how strongholds are formed.

The word of God says out of the heart the mouth speaks. When we begin to articulate what is in our hearts, actions soon follow. The Bible exhorts us to take every thought captive and bring it into the obedience of Christ[45].

For this is reason, I exhort intercessors to examine themselves regularly. Self-examination does not mean to dig up areas in our lives God has already dealt with, but to simply ask the Lord if there is something He wants to deal with in our heart. If the Lord highlights an area, it is time for this area to be cleansed and healed. For the intercessors especially, this is an on-going process. It is particularly important to seek the Lord about the following areas in preparing your heart to intercede.

Pride

Pride is the area of life that I ask intercessors to be the most watchful. Pride is the sin that caused Satan to fall. Pride is always crouching at the door. In fact, I have purposed never say to myself that pride is an area that I have already dealt with. Pride is very subtle and can creep into our lives undetected. So, I encourage our intercessors to be on watch especially for pride in their own lives[46].

Fear

Fear is another area to be aware of. Fear tries to paralyze us by tempting us to see situations and circumstances as bigger

---

[45] 2 Corinthians 10:5
[46] Reference Chapter 6

than God's ability to overcome. It is really a subtle form of idolatry. It is idolatry because what you magnify in your own eyes can be a form of worship, depending on the amount of attention you give to fear rather than remaining focused on God.

I went through a season about twenty years ago when God was dealing with the spirit of fear in my life. The particular fear I was battling was an intense fear of the dark. During that time, I was visiting my family in California for Christmas and I had to share a room with my aunt. Because of my fear, I wanted a light left on in the room but my aunt wanted the light turned off. So I lay awake for what seemed like several hours absolutely paralyzed with fear. Finally, when I could not stand it anymore, I went into the bathroom, just so I could turn on a light.

Amazingly, God spoke to me while I was in the bathroom. What the Lord said in those moments both convicted me and set me on a course of healing. He said, "Ellen, you fear this fear of the dark more than you fear me." Seeing my fear from God's perspective helped me to recognize that I needed to repent. My sin was in thinking that fear held more power than God's ability to protect me. I had agreed with the spirit of fear in how I was interpreting my environment.

Through this experience, I learned an important lesson for intercession. I cannot exercise authority over a demonic spirit unless I have examined myself and repented of wherever I may have agreed with its lie in my own life.

Practicing Proper Stewardship

One of the things I try to impress upon prophetic intercessors is to be a good steward of the prophetic gifts they have been given. The definition of stewardship is the responsibility to manage something belonging to another person. Essentially our spiritual gifts are given to us by God for the specific purpose of not only strengthening the church, but also as necessary tools needed in reaching the lost. One of the enemies of good stewardship is fear. Matthew 25 is a good example, in principle, of the importance of proper stewardship.

"Then he who had received the one talent came and said, 'Lord, I knew you to be a hard man, reaping where you have not sown, and gathering where you have not scattered seed. And I was afraid, and went and hid your talent in the ground. Look, there you have what is yours.' But his Lord answered and said to him, 'You wicked and lazy servant, you knew that I reap where I have not sown, and gather where I have not scattered seed. So you ought to have deposited my money with the bankers, and at my coming I would have received back my own with interest." Matthew 25:24-27

Fear should never be a reason for not sharing a prophetic word or sense. Our spiritual gifts are entrusted to us by God and we need to be faithful managers of their proper use.

Part of being a good steward has to do with our attitude in the expression of the spiritual gifts. We should never allow impatience to characterize our delivery of a prophetic word. Along with this, it is also important that we honor the body of Christ in the proper exercise of our prophetic gifts. The Bible is very clear that prophecy is subject to the prophet, which means that we have the ability to exercise self-control in the release of a prophetic word[47].

Discernment versus Criticism

We also need to be on guard about how we distinguish between prophetic discernment and criticism. There is a very fine line between the two. As intercessors, we must be particularly careful not to allow what we discern to become criticism. If the Lord reveals something negative about person or situation, it is usually entrusted to us for the purpose of intercession.

We must learn to see from God's perspective and resist the temptation to become judgmental or critical. Sometimes our greatest test comes when the Lord has just finished dealing with us in an area of our own wrong attitude or behavior. The test comes when we then encounter a brother or sister who is exhibiting that same wrong attitude. The temptation is to feel very self-righteous and then become critical of that person's fault—the one that we just gained victory over. We mistakenly think that God no longer needs to deal with us in that area of sin. Yet, God is continuing to refine us as he tests our reaction

---

[47] 1 Corinthians 14:32 NKJV

to a brother or sister manifesting the same fault. Is our response toward them one of love and compassion when we see them in error or are we judgmental? This is what I call the *Twice Refined Principle.* God wants to do more than cleanse us of sin. He wants our response to the faults of others to be one of love and compassion as well.

"But God demonstrates His own love toward us, in that while we were yet sinners, Christ died for us."   Romans 5:8

If we are to truly intercede with the heart of the Lord, we must learn see past people's faults and ask the Lord's wisdom about how He would have us pray for them.

Finally, leave a little room for people to grow past your perception of them. Often people, in our interactions with them, will live up to our expectation of them. It is important to not limit people or the circumstances we face with our own human reasoning. Our God is in the business of redeeming. There is no sin too great that God's love and redemptive power cannot reach. As intercessors, we must carry this perspective in our view of others and in the challenges we encounter.

"Now to him that is able to do exceedingly abundantly above all we ask or think, according to the power that works in us, to Him be the glory in the church by Christ Jesus to all generations, forever and ever. Amen"   Ephesians 3:20

Lean Not to Your Own Understanding

Proper stewardship of our prophetic gifts also involves being careful not to rely on your own understanding of a prophecy, but to seek the Lord in processing its meaning. As prophetic intercessors, we must be careful not to pray our own will into a person's life or circumstances, but seek the Lord for His will and then pray in agreement with it. Praying manipulative or controlling prayers for things that are outside of the will of God can become a form of what I call charismatic witchcraft[48].

The Matter of Delivery

Proper stewardship also has to do with how we deliver a prophetic word. When we receive a word from the Lord through the gift of prophecy, we need to declare the word exactly as the Lord gives it. A person functioning in this gift is hearing words from the Lord in their spirit that they are to simply repeat. Be careful not to change or alter a word received in this fashion. Doing so can have dramatic effects on how a person receives and understands what the Lord is speaking to them.

I had a friend who functioned strongly in the gift of prophecy. She had received a prophecy in which she thought one of the words used would sound too harsh, so my friend changed it. As my friend gave the prophecy to a certain woman, the woman had a puzzled look on her face and left. Later, my friend felt very convicted by the Lord because she had not given the

---

[48] See Chapter 6

prophecy in the way the Lord had given it to her. The next time she saw the woman she apologized and gave her the correct version of the prophecy. Instantly the woman had understanding and expressed her gratitude. My friend learned an important lesson that when operating in the gift of prophecy, it is important to give the word the way the Lord gave it. Even changing one word can make a difference.

With the other revelation gifts—word of knowledge, word of wisdom, and discernment of spirits—there is a little more flexibility in how these prophetic gifts are delivered because of the seer aspect or sensing associated with these prophetic expressions. When someone experiences a vision, describing what we see is an attempt to articulate what we perceive. We may get an overall sense of what the Lord is communicating, but trying to articulate what is seen is not always exact. The same is true with a dream. There may be many symbols in the dream that we need to seek the Lord about in understanding its meaning. An impression is a vague sensing in which we may struggle to find the right words to clearly describe what we perceive. In these cases we may find ourselves over explaining as we attempt to articulate as accurately as possible what we see or sense.

A Spiritual Compass

The last area of stewardship is to always allow the Bible to be your spiritual compass in processing and judging a prophetic word. Prophetic intercessors can get off track quickly when their revelation does not align with the word of God. We must also be willing to submit our revelation with a humble heart to those God has entrusted as our spiritual authority. If you are going to engage in any significant warfare or prophetic expression, it is important to stay under the oversight and guidance of your local church leadership.

Spiritual Seasons

From time to time, prophetic intercessors may experience a season where they feel like their prophetic gift is not flowing the way it used to. In fact, some intercessors may feel like the prophetic gift has completely shut off. It really has not, but it can feel that way. For those with the gift of discernment of spirits like me, these seasons feel like the lights have been turned out because of the ability to sense the spiritual atmosphere during these times is not as clear. It can actually feel very disorientating and the temptation is to feel very unspiritual.

Personally, I have experienced several of these seasons. Sometimes it has been a season of just a few weeks, other times months, and in rare cases years. When I first moved back to my home state of California in 1996, I went through a season of diminished discernment for almost two years. But I now can look back and see how the Lord was preparing me for a greater release of my prophetic gift and ministry calling.

I have learned to recognize that dry seasons are special times of equipping where God is imparting a greater release of the Holy Spirit to flow in and through my life. Often times these seasons are also followed by a time of promotion or an ability to flow at a stronger level in the prophetic. I have learned to recognize these times as seasons of spiritual growth and maturity, although it often feels like just the opposite is happening.

In fact, it can be a very awkward time where you find you are not responding like your normal self and saying things you should not. When I find myself in a restricted season, I have chosen to see it as a reminder that my spiritual gifts are not my identity. Rather, my identity is in Christ. I find it helpful to give yourself some grace and allow the Lord to draw you into a greater intimacy with Him. When you finally emerge from a restricted season, you will be amazed how the Holy Spirit flows through your life in a more powerful way. I have even caught myself saying at these times, "Wow, where did that come from?"

Setting the right Priorities

I have found over the years that most intercessors discover that they are not content to only be on a prayer team. There seems to be an unspoken tension between committing to a prayer team and wanting to be involved in more of the outreach portion of ministry. This actually is a natural progression in the lives of most intercessors. The prayer burden that the Lord gives an intercessor should lead them to want to be involved in more of a hands-on ministry. The difficulty comes in when people become over-committed in their ministry involvement. I usually recommend that if you know your primary call is as an intercessory leader or as a prayer warrior, then it is important to make prayer a priority when considering other opportunities for ministry. On the flip side, ministry involvement should also contain a heart for prayer, whether or not you are on a prayer team. I find that when people are over-involved, they experience burnout and are less effective. So it is important that you know what the Lord is requiring of you in giving your time and energy in the work of the ministry.

In Conclusion

The real secret to effective intercession is in developing an intimacy with the Lord and discerning the burden on His heart. In this personal time with our heavenly Father we begin to know His mind, His will, and His emotions concerning the people and circumstances we encounter.

From Genesis to Revelation we can see a master plan unfold with God's primary goal to redeem mankind. As intercessors, we must understand that redemption is at the very core of God's heart and is the motivation for all He does. Those called to intercession must embrace this perspective in order to properly intercede, along with submitting themselves to a process of examination and cleansing.

It is amazing how God will transform our heart, our attitude, and our perspective of others when we allow God to reveal and impart His redemptive heart for mankind. In this quiet time with the Father, we will soon discover our own heart begin to swell with compassion for others and a burden to pray!

Mentoring the Prophetic Intercessor Part II

"Blessed be the Lord my Rock, who trains my hands for war and my fingers for battle."   *Psalm 144:1*

Understanding God's heart for intercession begins with embracing His compassion for lost souls. In order to reach those in darkness we must understand that we live in a war zone. This is the reality of our earthly existence. The battle is over lost souls with a very real enemy opposing the church at every opportunity. With this in mind and as part of the mentoring process, I would like to share a biblical understanding of the battle we face and how to engage in effective spiritual warfare.

The Importance of a United Vision—Nehemiah's Story

The book of Nehemiah is a great picture of the kind of warfare encountered by the body of Christ and the importance of prayer when attempting to move forward in a united vision. It is also a wonderful illustration of how the Church can work together in unity to counter the opposition.

Nehemiah, upon hearing that the wall of Jerusalem had been broken down, wept and mourned for many days, seeking the

Lord in fasting and prayer about the matter. It was in this place of prayer that Nehemiah was granted favor and an assignment from the Lord to rebuild the walls of Jerusalem[49].

God often births vision out of those areas in our society where the walls have been broken down. Figuratively, these *broken down walls* are places where injustices, sin, and corruption have infiltrated a city or a nation. Because God's heart is always to restore, He will search for someone willing to receive His burden and plans to bring about restoration.

"The people of the land have used oppressions, committed robbery, and mistreated the poor and needy; and they wrongfully oppress the stranger. So I sought for a man among them who would make a wall, and stand in the gap before Me on behalf of the land, that I should not destroy it; but I found no one."   *Ezekiel 22:29-30*

This passage in Ezekiel reveals God's redemptive heart in response to sin running rampant in the city of Jerusalem and among His people. His response involved looking for one person who would be willing to stand in the gap. As we discussed earlier, a gap is a place where there is a breech in either a physical or spiritual wall. Without someone to stand in this place, this gap becomes a vulnerable place for an enemy invasion. So God looks for those willing to make up a wall of protection in prayer while the restoration is in process. This was

---

[49] Nehemiah 1; 2:5

happening in the book of Nehemiah. God was raising up Nehemiah to repair the walls of Jerusalem that were broken down because of Israel's disobedience.

Whenever God raises up a leader with a God-inspired vision, we can always expect opposition. Why? Because within every God-breathed assignment is a restorative purpose that advances the kingdom of God—light begins to overtake where darkness has been entrenched. When the kingdom of God advances, it severely limits the demonic opposition at work over a person or a geographic area. What is the result? The powers of darkness holding people in deception and bondage begin to lose their power to influence and the lost become much more open to receiving the gospel.

One thing we can learn from the book of Nehemiah is the importance of remaining focused on the assignment God has given us and not allowing demonic opposition to distract or stop us. Nehemiah could only do this by continually seeking God in prayer throughout every phase of his assignment.

Nehemiah's main opponents, Sanballat and Tobiah, were demonically influenced to oppose the rebuilding of the walls. Together these enemies conspired several plans of attack to either stop or slow down the work of rebuilding. Each time these enemies unleashed a new scheme Nehemiah prayed and was able to respond in wisdom to counter each assault.

The types of demonic strategies Nehemiah faced were false accusations, deception, fear, threat of invasion, confusion, distractions, internal strife among the people, and word curses[50]. Do these strategies sound similar to the types of opposition we encounter as well?

Instead of reacting Nehemiah sought the Lord in prayer to gain insight about the best way to respond. Nehemiah's response is an amazing example of what to do when we find ourselves in similar circumstances. When he was mocked and despised, Nehemiah rebuked Sanballat and Tobiah with the truth[51]. When dealing with word curses, Nehemiah countered by entering into personal intercession[52]. When there was a threat of invasion to cause fear and confusion, Nehemiah was given a strategy to set a watch and then wisdom about how to position the people along the wall so that the work could continue unhindered[53]. When there was a conspiracy to distract him, Nehemiah refused to be distracted or step away from his assignment[54]. Even when a false prophet was sent to deceive him, the Lord granted Nehemiah the ability to discern the deception.

"Then I perceived that God had not sent him at all, but that he had pronounced this prophecy against me because Sanballat and Tobiah had hired him."   *Nehemiah 6:12*

---

[50] Nehemiah 2:19-20; 4:3-4, 7-8; 6:2-11
[51] Nehemiah 2:20
[52] Nehemiah 4:4
[53] Nehemiah 4:7-13
[54] Nehemiah 6:3

Throughout the rebuilding of the walls, Nehemiah was confronted with continual opposition. Each time Nehemiah was given the wisdom and the strategy of the Lord in how to deal with it. The wisdom and discernment granted to Nehemiah was imparted to him as he sought the Lord in prayer.

When God has given us a vision, personally or corporately, we need to do the same. For a corporate or regional vision, as in the case of Nehemiah, the strength of all the people was necessary in executing the vision. Those positioned along the wall were called both to watch and to pray so that the burden of the task would not fall too heavily in either role. Likewise, as the body of Christ, we all have a role to play in the area of prayer as well as a call to build in reaching the lost. This is because we are all part of the same army. Even though there may be differing assignments and positions within the body of Christ, there are some responsibilities we all share—the great commission and the call to prayer. This is because prayer is the foundation for all effective ministry. It is where we receive God's wisdom and His plan of how to reach the lost. Prayer and evangelism are inseparable mandates in which both are necessary in order move in accordance to the prompting and timing of the Holy Spirit. We must remember that God does have a plan and a timing for what He desires to accomplish in and through us. Jesus revealed this concept when he stated that He himself only did what He saw the Father doing. In other words, Jesus' ministry direction was guided by what he discerned was on the Father's heart to accomplish.

Warfare Prayer

As discussed, moving forward in the will and direction of the Lord will involve spiritual opposition. In order to engage in effective spiritual warfare, an intercessor must clearly understand his or her position and authority in Christ. According to the book of Ephesians, we are seated with Christ in heavenly places. This is a critical understanding when we consider our spiritual walk, the warfare we experience, and how we are called to stand.

Let's begin by discussing the context of the battle we face and the nature of our warfare.

"v10 Finally, my brethren, be strong in the Lord, and in the power of his might. v11 Put on the whole armor of God, that you may be able to stand against the wiles of the devil. v12 For we wrestle not against flesh and blood, but against principalities, against powers, against rulers of the darkness of this world, against spiritual wickedness[55] in high places.[56] v13 Wherefore take unto you the whole armor of God, that you may be able to withstand in the evil day, and having done all to stand." Ephesians 6:10-13

---

[55] wicked spirits
[56] heavenly places

The context of this passage is that Paul has just finished giving the believers instructions on how to live a life pleasing to their heavenly Father. Paul recognizes that the believers will experience spiritual opposition and so his final exhortation is to become strong in the strength of the Lord[57].

How can God's people increase in the strength of the Lord? Verse 11 answers this question by instructing believers to put on the whole armor of God. The whole armor refers to both offensive and defensive weapons given to us by God for victory in a spiritual battle.

What kind of opposition do we face? This passage identifies our spiritual opposition as *the wiles of the devil.* The word *wiles* means methods or stratagems that are carefully planned by the enemy to tempt us into sin. These methods are hidden like ambushes in the circumstances we face and include sudden or impulsive thoughts to do wrong, hindrances or obstacles, discouragement, fears, lies or deception, sickness, word curses activated through murmuring, complaining, gossip, or slander spoken yourself or spoken by another person about you. We may encounter other types of opposition such as harassing or tormenting thoughts, nightmares, confusion, temptations, doubts or unbelief, oppression, depression, or a spirit of heaviness.

---

[57] verse 10

Paul explains in verse 13 that the real battle is not with flesh and blood[58], but against principalities[59], powers[60], rulers of the darkness of this world[61], and spiritual wickedness[62] in high places. All of this essentially shows us the demonic ranks of opposition organized against us by the devil.

What is the enemy seeking in these attacks? The devil seeks to bring about various divisions. His ultimate strategy is to separate us from God. So the devil opposes salvation by orchestrating various schemes to divide people in his effort to resist the advancement of the gospel. The following are three primary areas of demonic opposition the devil targets in order to bring division.

Opposes individual believers

The first area he targets in attempt to slow down the spread of the gospel is by diverting the attention of believers from their God-given assignment which is the great commission. Demonic opposition does this by sowing seeds of doubts, fears, unbelief, and offenses as it relates to our life circumstances.

Opposes covenant relationships

The second area the devil targets to oppose is covenant relationships. These Godly relationships are not limited to marriage. They also include ministry relationships, friendships,

---

[58] mankind
[59] a type leader in the demonic ranks
[60] evil powers opposing Christ
[61] who oversee geographical areas or regions
[62] wicked spirits

parents, and children. Whenever we encounter a relational conflict we need to ask ourselves, "What is the devil really after here?" Usually in a covenant relationship there is a divine purpose for that relationship, a plan that God intends to fulfill through the connection of specific individuals. In order to hinder God's plans, the devil opposes covenant relationships very strongly. We must be on guard for the strategies that would try to divide and separate these relationships. What is really at stake are the purposes of God being fulfilled in and through His people.

Opposes the church

The final area that the enemy seeks to divide is the church. The devil knows and is afraid of a united church. The promise in scripture is that the gates of hell will not prevail against a united church. This is why the devil works so hard to try and bring strife and division among the body of Christ. The devil knows that a united church with a God given assignment to advance the Kingdom is an unstoppable force; this is what causes the devil to tremble!

What is our best defense? Our best defense is in putting on the whole armor of God. This armor is available to us in Christ, so we can withstand (oppose or stand against) the wiles of the devil in what scripture calls *"the evil day."* What evil day is the scripture referring to? This phrase refers to the day that you are tempted or assaulted by these demonic schemes or surprise attacks.

The Armor of God

The armor of God that we are instructed to put on is found in Ephesians and is made up of six pieces: the Girdle of Truth, the Breastplate of Righteousness, Feet Shod with the Gospel of Peace, the Shield of Faith, the Helmet of Salvation, and the Sword of the Spirit. Each part of this armor has a unique role in providing a good defense against the strategies of the enemy as well as to wage spiritual warfare effectively[63].

When this passage in Ephesians was written, Paul's point of reference to military clothing was the Roman Soldier. So this is how the armor is described.

The Girdle of Truth

The first piece of armor is the Girdle of Truth. This was a leather apron that encircled a soldier's waist and held the sheath for a Sword, in this context we are referring to the Sword of the Spirit. Truth and the Word of God are always connected. The spiritual significance of the girdle is that truth inside protects the heart and mind. Truth has the ability to reveal right from wrong and reveal our position in relationship to truth. Truth also provides support to know where we stand in relation to God and all opposing forces. When truth is embraced, it has the ability to set us free from the power of sin and also grants us firm principles upon which to stand. The

---

[63] See What to Wear to War by Warren W. Wiersbe for resource information on the Armor of God

Girdle of Truth has the ability to hold things together so we have a greater freedom to move forward.

Picture for a moment a Roman soldier dressed in long flowing robes that extend down a little past his knees. Wearing only this robe would make running in battle quite a challenge. So a soldier tucked part of his garment into his leather apron. This freed the soldier's legs to run unencumbered. It is a good illustration of how truth impacts our lives. Truth frees us from areas of sin that could hinder us.

The Breastplate of Righteousness

The second piece of the armor is the Breastplate of Righteousness. The typical Breastplate was a coat of mail designed to cover the vital organs such as the heart and lungs. A coat of mail is made of thin strips of metal that are interwoven in multiple layers like a piece of fabric so that the thrust of a sword cannot penetrate.

The Breastplate of Righteousness symbolizes how we now wear the righteousness of Christ. When we wear Christ's righteousness and the Father looks at us, he no longer sees our sins and imperfections. Instead He sees the redeeming blood of His son Jesus covering us. This piece of the armor is a declaration of our acceptance before the Father, an approval that no demon has the authority to oppose. It is the righteousness of Christ that silences the accuser and dismantles Satan's opposition through his spoken accusations.

So when the enemy accuses or condemns us, we know that we can rebuke those thoughts confidently because of our right standing before God the Father.

The Gospel of Peace

The third piece of armor has to do with how our Feet are Shod with the Preparation of the Gospel of Peace. Roman soldiers wore sandals with leather straps bound to each sandal and then laced in a crisscrossed pattern on the calves. The bottom of each sandal was spiked so that the soldier could gain traction.

The spiritual significance of the sandals is that the gospel represents peace between God and man. When someone has received and embraced the gospel message, the result is peace with God. This peace allows us to establish a firm footing in our lives. As believers, we have automatically been deputized as God's ambassadors of peace to those who do not know God. This is the message we are sent to deliver to those who live in darkness.

The Shield of Faith

The next piece of armor is the Shield of Faith. To the Roman soldier a shield was a large wood frame with leather covering that was large enough to hide behind. The leather covering could be dipped in water to extinguish any fiery darts launched at a soldier. The fiery darts aimed at Christians are thoughts or words such as accusations, mocking, fears, doubts, and sudden thoughts to do wrong. The main purpose of these darts is to wound and torment the soul. When the Shield of Faith is in place, these darts cannot penetrate a person's life. What is it about faith that protects? Let's look at Psalm 91 to gain some insight.

"He will shield you with His wings. He will shelter you with His feathers. His faithful promises are your armor and protection."

Psalm 91:4 (NLT)

There is a very strong link in this passage between God's faithful promises and a person's armor and protection. In other words, what He has spoken as a promise to us carries the power to protect us until the promise is fulfilled. The Shield of Faith is activated in our lives when we mix our faith with the prophetic words of promise that God has declared over us. When our trust is firmly resting on the Lord for every detail of our lives, any and all fiery darts can quickly be extinguished or deflected.

When we face difficult situations or spiritual attack, we must activate this shield in order stand in the midst of adversity. A sobering passage in Isaiah declares this spiritual reality.

"Unless your faith is firm, I cannot cause you to stand firm."

Isaiah 7:9

In this verse the news of an approaching army brought great fear to the King of Jerusalem. In response, God sent Isaiah to comfort the king by prophesying to him that there is no reason to fear an invasion. Immediately after the promise, verse nine follows with an exhortation and a warning to the king that unless he learns to believe what the Lord has spoken, God will not cause him to stand firm. In fact, the king's unbelief carries the potential for the enemy to bring about his ruin.

Why is this true even though God has promised to protect him? Unbelief is like a broken down wall in one's life that gives the enemy access. God is offering the king complete protection if he will simply trust in His promises. The only thing that the Lord required of the king was a belief in what God had spoken. This is true for us as well. Believing in the promises of God is a choice. When we make a decision to place our confidence in God regardless of the circumstances, a shield of protection is activated as we agree for the fulfillment of His promises.

The Helmet of Salvation

The fifth piece of armor is the Helmet of Salvation. The Roman soldier wore a metal helmet to protect his head from attacks. The spiritual correlation for us is that this helmet protects our minds. As we have already touched on, the mind is the real battlefield for most demonic attack. The devil knows that whatever we meditate on will eventually become an action. We must be very careful to guard our thought life. In order for this piece of the armor to be set into place, you must first repent of your sins and receive the salvation of the Lord.

Ellen Laitinen

The Sword of the Spirit

The last piece of the armor is the Sword of the Spirit. This is the only part of the armor that is both an offensive and defensive weapon. The holder for this sword, the sheath, is also strategically located in the girdle of truth. The Word of God and truth are inseparable. Hebrews 4:12 reveals that the Sword of the Spirit is a two-edged sword, alive and powerful, that can defend by separating truth from error and dismantling lies. Also the sword is used offensively when the Word God is shared and lost souls are set free.

Our positional authority to use these weapons is based on the fact that we are co-heirs with Christ[64]. From this perspective, we must understand that our position in a spiritual battle is to wage warfare with the authority Christ gave us. All six pieces of the armor are given to enable us to stand firm and secure victory within the battles we encounter. This is why it is important to have a working knowledge of the spiritual weapons we've been given in Christ.

"For the weapons of our warfare are not carnal but mighty in God for the pulling down of strongholds, casting down arguments and every high thing that exalts itself against the knowledge of God, bringing every thought into captivity to the obedience of Christ."　　　　　*2 Corinthians 10:4-5*

---

[64] Ephesians 2:6

Responding to Spiritual Attack

In spiritual warfare there is a principle of strength versus authority involved in responding to a spiritual attack. Most of the attacks we experience as believers are the fiery darts, in the form of thoughts, that are the devil's attempt to weaken our faith and cause us to move into fear or unbelief. When our faith and confidence are shaken, it is a challenge to remain focused on our God-given assignment. When we focus on ourselves and how we feel, and it becomes very difficult to see anything beyond ourselves. The Bible teaches that spiritual attacks will come and that we are to respond by standing strong in the Lord and in the power of His might[65].

Responding versus Reacting

When confronted with spiritual attack, I encourage intercessors to resist the temptation to react. We can avoid reacting by taking a moment to seek God before we respond. In doing so, we position ourselves to hear God and gain spiritual insight in correctly discerning the battle. Then we can use our God-given authority to break the power of the assault. This is step one, gaining the Lord's perspective.

Power in Agreement

If the warfare continues it may be because of the strength of the opposition. Step two involves asking a brother or sister in Christ to agree with us in prayer in order to break the power of

---

[65] Ephesians 6:10 NKJV

the attack. There is a multiplication principle of spiritual strength when we join with other believers. Before an intercessor asks for prayer, I encourage him or her to seek the Lord for a scripture to stand on in the midst of the battle. Then when they go to ask for prayer, they have already developed a sense of what the Lord is saying and just need another brother or sister to agree with them in faith. I encourage this practice so that intercessors learn to hear the Lord in the midst of opposition rather than first running to another believer for help. It is vital for an intercessor to develop their own spiritual muscles of faith by using the authority they have been given in Christ. When step two has been exercised and the opposition continues, the warfare is often about authority rather than strength.

Positional Authority

Step three involves contacting someone in spiritual authority over you to pray, such as a home-fellowship leader, elder, pastor, Christian parent, and so on. Although the first three steps are mostly what we deal with when we experience spiritual warfare, there are times when the spiritual opposition may require both the strength of a group of believers as well as involving someone in spiritual authority.

I learned this principle of strength versus authority when I was living in Vermont. I was home sick one day from work when I started to experience a severe blurring of vision in both of my eyes. This blurry vision came on so suddenly that I suspected it was a demonic assault rather than a physical condition. My initial response was to rebuke it, but the condition grew worse. So I decided to call a sister in Christ and ask her for prayer. When we prayed, the attack still did not break. By then my vision was so blurry that I could not read the numbers on the phone in front of me. I literally had to dial by remembering the position of the numbers on the phone. Consequently, I was feeling very afraid and was not sure what to do.

When I finished praying with my friend, I had a strong impression to call my senior pastor. So I dialed the church office and amazingly was able to speak with my senior pastor immediately. I felt a little awkward asking for prayer for blurry vision because I thought for sure my pastor would think I was a little strange. However, because my vision was impaired and I desperately needed the prayer, I pushed past my hesitation and called. Of course my pastor was very gracious in spite of this unusual request. Amazingly, when he began to pray, the attack broke and my vision was instantly restored.

The reason I teach this three-step principle is that it is important not to run to our leadership every time we experience a spiritual attack. We have authority God has given us that we need to exercise and not develop an unhealthy dependency on others. With this said, it is also important to recognize that there are different strengths and authority levels involved in spiritual warfare and at times it is necessary to involve other believers as well as leaders when we are experiencing strong warfare.

Ellen Laitinen

On our prophetic intercession team, we each have prayer buddies with whom we check in weekly. I have asked everyone on the team to be sure to follow this three step process. That means, after step two, I should be receiving a call. Usually I will ask the team during our meetings how they are doing and if they are sensing any warfare. This survey is important for a couple of reasons.

1. As the team leader, I want to know how the intercessors are doing personally. As prophetic intercessors with an assignment to pray protection and advancement of the church vision, we are essentially standing on the front lines of the battlefield.

2. There is often a pattern of how the team is experiencing spiritual attack. Consistently, I have found that when the intercessors experience spiritual opposition such as infirmity, confusion, fears, discouragement, distractions, etc., this same opposition is also attacking the church.

I encourage our intercessors to be careful to not focus in on themselves when they experience spiritual warfare, especially when an attack tempts us to react on an emotional level. The devil knows that prophetic intercessors have the kind of spiritual gifts that enable us to discern demonic strategies. That is why so much of the spiritual attack that intercessors experience can be emotionally based with thoughts of rejection, fear, discouragement, isolation, and anger. At times, intercessors are challenged circumstantially through the words, actions, and attitudes of other people that may have a demonic stratagem behind them designed to distract or create a façade of a situation or relational interaction that is not based on the truth.

As intercessors, we have to discipline ourselves to look past the temptation to feel sorry for ourselves or get caught up in emotions that will only distract us from maintaining our prayer assignment. Allowing God to deal with areas of our mind, will, and emotions is critical in preparing us to stand firm in the place of intercession. If we have places of sin, un-forgiveness, unbelief, or emotional pain that we are not willing to yield to the Lord, we will experience difficulty in maintaining our prayer watch.

Dreams

Occasionally intercessors experience warfare in the middle of the night. They may suddenly awaken with a strong sense of fear or oppression. It could be following a dream or something they are discerning. If a dream has caused these negative emotions, the dream is usually not from the Lord. It is important to pay attention to the feeling that accompanies dreams because the feeling is often an indicator of whether the dream is truly from the Lord or not. Dreams that leave you with a sense of fear, confusion, dread, anger, or oppression are not of the Lord and the spirit behind these dreams needs to be rebuked. However, some dreams are a warning and could initially cause fear because of the urgency of the revelation. However this kind of fear has to do with the fear of the Lord, not a spirit of fear.

"God has not given a spirit of fear but of love, of power and a sound mind."   *2 Timothy 1:7*

I have had some dreams in which I felt my spirit battling while I was asleep. Because of these dreams, I have taught myself how to war even while asleep. Sometimes I have experienced demonic attacks where I have awakened and not been able to move or talk. In those situations, when I am in a semi-unconscious state, I plead the blood of Jesus in my thoughts. When I have done this, the attack breaks.

As a preventative measure, I have found that I can speak to my soul and declare aloud, "If I experience any demonic dream or nightmare in the night season, I will plead the blood of Jesus and rebuke it," Amazingly, I find myself responding this way while I am asleep. Let me be clear, I am not recommending that you say this to yourself every night. Instead have this stance as a resolve in your mind, so if there is any demonic attack in your dreams that you will plead the blood and rebuke it. Please understand that I do not seek to engage in spiritual warfare at night, I much prefer to get a good night's rest.

Three-Second Rule

At times, I have suddenly awakened in the middle of the night with a strong sense of fear. Over time I have learned that I do not have to agree with the fear I sense. A spirit of fear comes in the form of a thought or a feeling that tries to convince me to be afraid. When I have suddenly awakened with a fearful thought, I discovered I have about three seconds to rebuke this fear before I begin reacting in fear. I affectionately call this the 3-second rule. I have not always recognized my choice to embrace fear or not. When I have reacted in fear after being suddenly awakened, I end up awake for several hours dealing with the fear before I am able to go back to sleep.

One night when this happened, I could sense the fear, but then I heard the voice of the Lord say, "Are you really afraid?" I thought about it and realized no, I did not feel afraid. Then the Lord said, "Rebuke the spirit of fear." When I did, it immediately fled and I was able to go back to sleep.

Since then, I very rarely ever wake up with a sense of fear. On the few occasions that I do, I rebuke fear and then make it a point to pray for everyone I can think of before I fall asleep. Needless to say, the enemy is not too anxious to use this strategy on me anymore.

One of the things I keep in mind is to not allow the enemy to dictate when I engage in spiritual warfare. When the enemy attacks, I take a moment to ask the Lord how or if I should respond. If I wake up at night with a burden from the Lord, then I take time to intercede. If I am just experiencing an attack, I rebuke it and go back to sleep.

Dealing with Witchcraft and Curses

Witchcraft involves accessing spiritual power of a demonic nature and outside the will of God that can adversely affect another person's life or situation. Witchcraft mostly takes the form of curses—words spoken to call down harm or evil on someone's life or circumstances. Words spoken with an evil intent can carry a demonic power that can become a harassing form of spiritual opposition.

When a word curse is in operation, people can experience hindrances in completing ordinary tasks or difficulties in using sound and communication equipment, such as phones, computers, e-mail and internet access, and fax machines. Other more severe indicators of witchcraft can include accidents or calamities, confusion or difficulty in thinking, sickness, an unnatural weariness, relational difficulties, and misunderstandings.

We must remember that we live in a spiritual war zone on this earth. Part of the warfare we encounter as Christians includes people involved in occult practices who are used by the devil to oppose the Church. There are people who actually curse Christians regularly. Some occult groups have specific times of the year when they issue specific curses and even fast and pray against Christian marriages, pastors and young people. It is important to remember God's perspective about this opposition.

"Like a flitting sparrow, like a flying swallow, so a curse without cause shall not alight." Proverbs 26:2

"No weapon formed against you shall prosper, and every tongue which rises up against you in judgment You will condemn. This is the heritage of the servants of the Lord and their righteousness is from me." Isaiah 54:17

"Having disarmed principalities and powers, He made a public spectacle of them, triumphing over them in it." Colossians 2:15

We learn from these passages that unless there is an open door of sin in our lives, a word curse cannot take root in our lives. A curse has no power to operate unless, when tempted, we agree with the lies. Instead, we should combat these demonic thoughts with truth and exercise our faith in the promises of God.

The New Testament is clear. Jesus has already defeated and stripped the authority of the demonic powers behind this kind of opposition. Remember, as co-heirs with Christ Jesus, we have been granted authority over all the power of the enemy. This does not mean that the enemy will not try to oppose us. Our adversary continues to operate illegally by attempting to formulate weapons and schemes against God's people. Through demonic lies and deception, he attacks our faith as a way to get us to agree with his demonic plan for our lives. So we need to be on guard and appropriate the authority we have been given in Christ when we see this illegal activity going on.

It is important to keep in mind that the primary reason for spiritual opposition has to do with the spread of the gospel in the earth. Jesus knew that the devil would oppose the Church which is why He gave authority over demons to his disciples.

"Then He called His twelve disciples together and gave them authority over all demons and to cure diseases. He sent them to preach the kingdom of God and to heal the sick."

Luke 9:1-2

How then should we deal with word curses when we discern them?

Step One: Be sure that we have not come into agreement with the lie that is opposing us. If we have agreed with the enemy's lies, then repent. The word of God then makes it very clear how to deal with those who would curse us:

"Bless those who curse you, and pray for those who despitefully use you."   *Luke 6:28*

Step Two: Bless the people who have cursed us. Remember, our real warfare is not against flesh and blood (people), but against demonic forces. We must not forget that Jesus died to redeem all those who are lost. That includes those who are involved in the occult.

Step Three: Break the power of the demonic strategy by declaring the blood of Jesus over the person or situation affected by these curses. Pleading the blood of Jesus establishes a boundary that separates demonic activity from operating in a person's life or situation.

Step Four: Because so much of what opposes us comes in the form of harassing thoughts, another step is to take every thought captive and bring it into the obedience of Christ. Then ask the Lord to reverse the effects of the demonic strategy. In doing so, our authority in Christ can then dismantle the strategy of the enemy when we declare the will of the Lord or apply the truth of His word.

Step Five: Pray for the salvation of those who would curse us. People who are speaking evil over the lives of others are in great need of our prayers. Especially people involved in the occult, they are often living in great emotional pain and desperately need God. When we discern this form of demonic activity, it should alert us to be praying for those who are bound by the enemy. The heart of the Lord is always to redeem and we must carry that mindset whenever we encounter spiritual opposition involving people.

Maintaining a Victory Mindset

Nehemiah was successful in his assignment because he maintained a victory mindset. We must do the same by learning how to abide in the stronghold of the Lord. This is our greatest defense! It is in this secret place of His presence that we can best hear the voice of the Lord, see our situations from His perspective and respond with His wisdom to our daily challenges. Learning to abide in His presence is a call to come up higher by allowing ourselves to be sensitive to the Holy Spirit's promptings and guidance when facing life's circumstances rather than wrestling with our own human reasoning. The following are some suggestions that I have found very helpful in learning to cultivate and abide in the Lord's presence.

Praise and Worship

A major key to coming into the presence of the Lord is by entering into heart-felt praise and worship. As we yield ourselves to declarations of praise, the Bible says that God inhabits, or is enthroned on, the praises of his people[66]. As the presence of the Lord is manifested, we then respond to His presence in worship. Fortunately, we are not limited to experiencing God's presence only at church with a full worship team. Whether or not you are musical, have a nice singing voice, play an instrument, write songs, or play worship CDs, remember that God is looking at the heart. He is pleased when we offer Him praise in whatever ability level we have been given. Practicing daily worship is vital to your spiritual refreshment.

I used to be on a worship team that traveled two times a month out of our local area. During those ministry times, we would experience such a strong presence of the Lord and God would

---

[66] Psalm 22:3

minister powerfully through our team. Following these weekend ministry times, most of us were physically exhausted on Monday morning when we had to return to work. So I asked the Lord for some wisdom in dealing with this weariness and He revealed a strategy to me that has been very effective. The Holy Spirit reminded me of the story of Jesus when the woman with the issue of blood reached out and touched the hem of Jesus' garment[67]. The way Jesus responded is interesting:

"And Jesus, immediately knowing in himself that power had gone out of Him, turned around and said, 'Who touched my clothes?'"   Mark 5:30

Like Jesus, when there is a strong anointing of God during times of ministry, supernatural power goes out from us. Because we are human, ministry can physically fatigue us afterwards. So the Lord showed me that if I played worship music or scripture throughout the night it would strengthen and refresh my spirit. Sure enough, it worked! When I played worship music all night after a weekend of intense ministry, I did not wake up Monday morning feeling exhausted.

Personal Communion

We can also enter into God's presence through our personal communion time with the Lord, not to be confused with intercession when we pray for others. Our personal communion time is where our relationship with God is developed and His

---

[67] Mark 5:27-29

presence is cultivated. It is the place we seek God through our personal times of prayer, reading the Word, and listening to what the Lord speaks to us in His still small voice. It is the time we cast our cares onto Him, inquire about our future direction, and sense the Holy Spirit's prompting as we begin our day. One way you can ensure this personal prayer time is by making a daily appointment with God and then be faithful to keep it!

The scriptures reveal in Hebrews 4:12 that the *"Word of God is living and active, sharper than a two-edged sword, dividing soul and spirit, truth and marrow; it judges the thoughts and attitudes of the heart."* As we read and meditate on His word, there is a separation going on in our heart that is adjusting, cleansing, and aligning us with God's truth. Our senior pastor, David Cannistraci, has frequently exhorted us to find scriptures to address weak areas in ourselves where we need to develop more of God's character and then meditate on these verses. In this way the Word of God can be at work within our thoughts and attitudes while the Lord is transforming our heart.

Setting a Regular Fast

Another key to coming into a greater intimacy with God is establishing a regular fasting day. When we refrain from eating or some other activity that brings pleasure or satisfaction to our flesh, this act of the fasting gives our spirit a heightened sensitivity to the direction of the Holy Spirit. Fasting is not only a key to entering into the presence of the Lord, but also in staying prophetically sensitive to the voice of the Lord when we pray or intercede. For this reason, I encourage all intercessors to set aside one day a week to fast. This can be an all day or partial day fast, however the Lord leads you.

So much in our daily lives can distract us and tempt us to battle in our souls. That is why we must abide in the presence of the Lord and learn to carry His presence with us throughout our day. Intercession involves standing in the gap to pray protection and restoration where the wall has been broken down in people's lives through sin or broken relationships. For us to stay effective in our intercession, we must learn to abide in the stronghold of the Lord.

Some Preventative Measures

In cultivating the presence of God in your life it is important to maintain right relationships in accordance to Matthew 18. Be sure to keep short accounts in your relationships by practicing forgiveness, confronting in love, and choosing to become offense-less.

In my family, my grandfather loved to identify the sore spots in different family members and say things to make them upset. I watched this pattern go on for several years as he targeted family member after family member. So when I was fifteen, I made a decision that I would never be offended by anything he said. Around that time, I became a Christian and made a decision not to drink alcohol. My decision was not based on religion. Actually, my reason was that some family members had an alcohol problem and I had witnessed the destructive pattern that resulted. My grandfather did not know this was my reason, but he observed that I always refused alcohol when it was offered.

Please understand, I came from a family where social drinking was encouraged at family parties. It was not unusual for many members of my family to come home and have a couple drinks every night after work. That is why my grandfather thought my behavior was odd. He began teasing me by making jokes about alcohol and then always made it a point to offer me a bourbon and soda. Fortunately, because I had made this decision to not be offended, I never was. His comments and jokes went on for many years, but it never impacted me. Ironically, the opposite occurred. My grandfather began to respect the fact that I was never offended by his comments and that I loved him unconditionally.

A life lesson I learned from my encounter with my grandfather was how we do have a choice about whether or not we are offended. I do not mean to make light of offenses. I realize that we wrestle with some offenses as a result of devastating circumstances. I wish I could say that I have not wrestled with being offended in other areas of my life. What we must understand is that the Bible warns us that offenses are unavoidable; however, it is our decision in how we respond.

"Woe to the world because of offenses! For offenses must come, but woe to that man by whom the offense comes!"

Matthew 18:7

The real danger of an offense is in its power to tempt someone to sin or to stumble in their response to the offense. This is why there is such a strong warning not to be a source of an offense to anyone. Ultimately, God will hold the offenders to account for their actions. As intercessors, it is critical that we not allow ourselves to be ensnared by offenses.

Rest for the Weary Warrior

It is amazing how your perspective of life can dramatically change when you are overtired and exhausted. As with everything that God gives us, we must be good stewards of our time. That includes getting enough rest so that our physical body can be refreshed.

As intercessors, one of the things that we must guard against is interceding past the point of exhaustion. Like all warriors, we need to allow ourselves a time of rest. For some intercessors, this is very difficult for them to do. Psalm 3 is a good illustration of David in the middle of battle and what he did in order to get some much needed rest.

"Lord, how they have increased who trouble me! Many are they that rise up against me. Many are they who say of me, 'There is no help for him in God.' Selah. But you, O Lord, area shield for me, my glory and the lifter of my head. I cried to the Lord with

my voice, and He heard me out of His Holy hill. Selah. I lay down and slept; I awoke, for the Lord sustained me."

Psalm 3:1-5

The context of this psalm is a battle scene in which enemy forces are increasing in numbers all around David. These enemies are mocking him by declaring that he is alone and that even God will not help him.

The word *Selah* following this taunting of the enemy is interesting—it means to pause and to look up. At this critical point of weariness, David pauses and looks up. In the face of utter exhaustion and growing opposition, David turns his focus upon the Lord and declares the faithfulness of God as his shield and the lifter of his head. As he continues to cry out, David is then filled with an assurance that God has indeed heard him.

The next verse is shocking when you consider the situation! David lies down and sleeps. Given his current circumstances, this is not exactly the time for a nap; David is in the middle of a battlefield.

Yet, God did become his shield to protect and sustain David while he was resting. In fact, God even took up the battle that brought about the complete demise of his enemies while David rested.

This is an amazing testimony of the level of trust David had in the Lord to watch over him. Upon awaking, David expresses his gratitude by giving glory to God for sustaining him in the midst of battle.

We have this same provision in Christ when we are feeling weary as well. Like David, we as intercessors can look to God to sustain us while we receive rest and refreshment. This may mean we turn our prayer burden over to the Lord for a time. When I am feeling weary I have learned to send what I call *arrow prayers* to God. This is where I quickly make mention of the person and ask the Lord to meet them at their point of need. What we learn from Psalm 3 is the secret to David's ability to rest depends on giving the battle over to the Lord, trusting God, and finding peace within His protective shield.

In Conclusion

Whenever the church advances in a united vision, we can expect spiritual opposition. Satan does not like to give up areas that He has been free to exercise illegal influence over the hearts and minds of people. Although Christ has already broken the power of sin and death at the cross, Jesus has chosen the church as his vehicle to advance the Kingdom until He returns once again. Therefore, we as believers have all been commissioned as His ambassadors of reconciliation with a responsibility to share this good news with others. It is for this reason we are also all called to pray. Prayer is a necessary ingredient if we want to experience effective ministry.

For those specifically called to prophetic intercession, it has been my hope to present a clear picture of the spiritual battle we encounter, what is at stake, how to utilize the weapons God has given us and how we can war with wisdom. This chapter was not intended to address every aspect of spiritual warfare nor exclude other intercessors who are not prophetic in their prayer expression. Rather, my objective has been to offer the foundational biblical perspectives necessary in the mentoring of a prophetic intercessor.

Chapter 5

Ellen Laitinen

Aligning with Pastoral Authority

"Everyone must submit himself to the governing authorities, for there is no authority except that which God has established. The authorities that exist have been established by God."

Romans 13:1-2

There is a great move among churches today in recognizing the value of prayer and integrating prayer as an integral part of the life flow of the local church. Many churches are at various stages of understanding how prayer is strongly linked to effective ministry. As the importance of prayer continues to emerge, the roles of prayer warriors, prophetic intercessors, and watchmen have yet to be realized and implemented fully. Although pastors are recognizing the value of intercessors and prophetic intercessors to a greater extent, there is an issue: How are pastors and intercessors supposed to relate to each other? Especially prophetic intercessors?

"From whom the whole body fitly joined together and compacted by that which every joint supplies, according to the effectual working in the measure of every part, makes increase of the body unto the edifying of itself in love."

Ephesians 4:16

Connecting to Pastoral Leadership

In order for prophetic intercessors to be truly effective in their ministry there must be healthy communication between them and their church leadership. One thing that hinders this relationship is a lack of understanding, on the part of many intercessors, of their true position in the authority structure of the church. Often this lack of understanding comes from a lack of instruction or an inconsistency in the body of Christ about what this relationship should be. Although there are differences from church to church, it is helpful for intercessors to understand some basic principles. For prophetic intercessors to blossom into the fullness of their intercessory call, there must be a clear understanding of headship and submission.

"And God placed all things under his feet and appointed him to be head over everything for the church." Ephesians 1:22 (NIV)

In this passage we can see how the Father extends His authority by appointing Jesus as head over the church. A further extension of this authority is the divine placement of those leaders called to be over us. Romans 13 reveals that no authority exists except from God. Therefore all existing authorities are appointed by God for the purpose of helping us.

"For rulers are not a terror to good works, but to evil. Do you want to be unafraid of the authority? Do what is good, and you will have praise from the same. For he is God's minister to you for good."   *Romans 13:3-4a*

Pastors are one form of authority God has provided for His church. When we choose to become part of a local church body, we are agreeing also to submit to the church leadership. It is important to note that God holds these shepherds to a higher level of accountability because of their responsibility. To underscore the seriousness of a pastoral calling, let us take a look at Ezekiel 34. The context for this passage is the Lord reprimanding the shepherds for taking care of themselves and not fulfilling their responsibility to the flock.

"Therefore, you shepherds, hear the word of the Lord. As surely as I live, declares the Sovereign Lord, because my flock lacks a shepherd and so has been plundered and has become food for all the wild animals, and because my shepherds did not search for my flock but cared for themselves rather than my flock, therefore, O shepherds, hear the word of the Lord: This is what the Sovereign Lord says: I am against the shepherds and will hold them accountable for my flock."

Ezekiel 34:7-10a (NIV)

The passage goes on to say how the Lord will execute judgment on these shepherds because of their wicked actions and rescue the afflicted sheep. It is very clear that while the Lord has entrusted shepherds with the oversight of a flock, He will also hold them accountable out of His love for the sheep. When there is wrongdoing, the flock is not designated by God to execute judgment or bring correction. That responsibility rests with the Lord and those with whom a pastor has a relationship of accountability, such as a board of elders, another pastor, or an apostle.

If the Lord has called you to serve in a particular church, then there is no mistake that the Lord has placed the pastor in authority over you. Whether or not you feel your pastor understands you or your spiritual gift has nothing to do with the fact that the pastor is the established authority. The pastor is actually God's gift to you and you can trust that God has put something in that pastor that you need to be equipped. The converse is true as well. You are placed in a particular church as an important part of its proper functioning.

"And He Himself gave some to be apostles, some prophets, some evangelists, and some pastors and teachers for the equipping of the saints for the work of the ministry, for the edifying of the body of Christ."   Ephesians 4:11-12

Right Attitudes

The first step in connecting properly to leadership begins with heart attitudes. As a prophetic intercessor, your approach in relating to your church leadership always should be characterized by an attitude of submission, humility, and servant-hood. Jesus himself said that he did not come to be served, but to serve.

In a healthy church, servant-hood should be a strong character trait among its members. This sounds easy until a conflict arises. When a conflict arises, the Lord will be faithful to move on your behalf if you will remember to stay in alignment with the proper authority structure and maintain a godly attitude. In resolving an issue, it is important to seek the Lord's wisdom. God may require you to humble yourself and repent or wait upon Him for the resolution. The Lord may need time to work in the heart of the other person to bring a healthy resolve. When there is an offense, you may need to confront the person in love as Matthew 18 exhorts.

"Moreover if your brother sins against you, go and tell him his fault between you and him alone. If he hears you then you have gained your brother."   *Matthew 18:15*

When there is an offense with a brother or church leadership, it is vitally important to maintain a posture of right standing in our attitudes and reactions before the Lord. God sees our heart, even when no one else does, and it is during conflicts that our character is proven. Although it does not always happen in the timing we prefer, be assured that when an injustice is done, God will move on our behalf. How can we be assured that the Lord will bring a just resolution, especially when leadership is involved? You can be confident because of the accountability in which the Lord holds his shepherds, an accountability that is motivated by God's love for his people.

Likewise, God also will hold his people accountable for their actions and responses. When intercessors allow themselves to react to situations with wrong attitudes, actions, or words, they step out of their position to pray effectively for the situation.

Why is this true? It happens because intercessors have reacted in the flesh, rather than the Spirit. In doing so, they've put themselves in a position of needing the Lord's discipline. When we have wrong attitudes in our relationships, it hinders our prayers. The following is a good example of this principle.

"Husbands, likewise, dwell with them with understanding, giving honor to the wife, as to the weaker vessel, and as being heirs together of the grace of life, that your prayers may not be hindered."   *1 Peter 3:7*

This particular scripture refers to husbands, but in effect, it really applies to all of us. It reveals we can do things that cause our prayers to be ineffective. The specific attitude addressed in this passage is a husband's lack of honor towards his wife. Although the context of this exhortation is the covenantal relationship of marriage, I believe this principle holds true in other relationships as well (that is, parents, family, friends, pastors, employers, co-workers, peers, government leaders, and all those in authority over us).

We need to place a greater importance on maintaining godly attitudes in our relationships than in our desire to be right! Why? It is because of the hindrances we can bring upon ourselves. Just imagine how wrong attitudes can impact the ministry of an intercessor!

The greatest failure that I have seen among intercessors is in their attitude towards church leadership—regardless of whether the intercessors are right or wrong in what they discern about leadership. Because of an intercessor's call to prayer, we cannot afford to allow ourselves to be critical or judgmental. Our position must always be one of grace and mercy. For this reason, we must be careful to avoid murmuring, gossip, slander, and complaining. These wrong attitudes and actions can render us ineffective in our prayer life.

Having said this, I know God must do a deeper refining of character in order to have godly responses. In addition to God bringing correction to our fleshly attitudes, we must realize that our warfare is not against flesh and blood, but against principalities, powers, and rulers of darkness in high places.

When a conflict arises in our relationships, we must begin to see that the real battle is not against a person. Ask yourself, "What is the enemy trying to ultimately accomplish through this conflict?" Many times the devil is trying to bring division between believers so that God's purpose for a relationship will not be accomplished. This is especially true of marriage and ministry relationships.

Please understand, I am not saying that people are not responsible for the things they say or do. We are still accountable before God for any wrong attitudes and actions in our treatment of others. However, we need to understand that the real battle is not with a person. There is a spiritual dimension to conflict that we must learn to recognize.

The deeper refining that God desires is in our response toward someone who has wronged us. Is our response one of love and compassion or anger and resentment? The minute we let ourselves react in the flesh, we are hindered from discerning the mind of Christ to pray for that situation. This is why it is particularly important for intercessors to be on guard against any temptation that would knock us out of our intercessory position!

I wish I could tell you that I am never challenged by conflict or that I have never had a wrong attitude, but that would not be true. Over time, I have learned to ask myself a question when I am confronted with hurtful situations or by negative thoughts tempting me to focus inwardly. I ask, "What am I not seeing because I am being tempted to feel sorry for myself?" Many times the purpose for a spiritual attack is as a diversionary tactic to get a prophetic intercessor off their watch. This is especially true for those intercessors have strong discernment and are called as watchmen. Because of their ability to discern the spiritual climate, the enemy tries hard to distract these intercessors from seeing what he is really doing. This is why it is so critical for intercessors to understand how effective intercession has everything to do with maintaining clean hands and a pure heart.

Understanding Our True Position

"That power is like the working of his mighty strength, which he exerted in Christ when he raised him from the dead and seated him at his right hand in the heavenly realms, far above all rule and authority, power and dominion, and every title that can be given, not only for the present age but also in the age to come. And God placed all things under his feet and appointed him to be head over everything for the church, which is his body, the fullness of him who fills everything in every way."

Ephesians 1:19b-23 (NIV)

Based on this initial understanding, Ephesians 2 goes on to clarify our unique position and the authority we've been given.

"And God raised us up with Christ and seated us with him in the heavenly realms in Christ Jesus."   *Ephesians 2:6*

What is the significance of our position as co-heirs with Christ Jesus? As a result of being raised up and seated with Christ, we have now been given His authority in the heavenly realms. This truth is evident when Jesus sent out the seventy-two workers.

"The seventy-two returned with joy and said, 'Lord even the demons submit to us in your name.'"   *Luke 10:17 (NIV)*

Jesus responds in verses 18-20 by saying:

"I saw Satan fall like lightning from heaven. I have given you authority to trample on snakes and scorpions and to overcome

all the power of the enemy; nothing will harm you. However, do not rejoice that the spirits submit to you, but rejoice that your names are written in heaven." Luke 10:18-20 (NIV)

Jesus clarifies the significance of this authority with a strong exhortation: *"Do not rejoice that the spirits submit to you, but rejoice that your names are written in heaven."*

Why does He caution his followers so strongly? Jesus knew that the proper exercise of this power must include an attitude of humility. The real enemy Christ warns about is pride and the best defense in guarding against pride is a humble heart. The posture of humility recognizes a need for God and acknowledges that He alone is the source of all authority, in heaven and on the earth. It is His authority on which we must rely. Our true position, as joint heirs with Christ, is based on the understanding that our authority is extended to us as part of the privilege of sonship.

Interestingly enough, most of the warfare we encounter as intercessors is an attack on our position in Christ. Satan knows that he cannot undo what Jesus has accomplished for us at Calvary. So, the next best thing is to devise schemes to render us ineffective. Actually the devil tries to make us ineffective by tempting us to respond inappropriately to our circumstances. We react rather than respond. That is why it is important to practice the biblical principles of love and forgiveness within our relationships. If we will obey the teachings of Jesus to love one another, walk in forgiveness, maintain an attitude of humility, and guard what we say, our obedience acts as shield to protect us from the schemes of the enemy.

Why is this so important? In spiritual warfare there are external and internal battles. When there is an enemy assault, it is better to only have to confront what is attacking externally. An external battle has to do with your life circumstances (job, finances, relationships, and so on) and the spiritual atmosphere influencing those situations. If there is sin in your heart, then the enemy has a foothold in your life and a legal right to harass you internally. Sin gives the enemy a legal right to accuse you. An internal battle has to do with your mind (thoughts), will (choices), emotions (feelings) and the attitudes and the actions they produce.

When a spiritual battle is both external and internal, the remedy is to settle the internal battle first. Settling the internal battle usually involves repenting of sin and then, because of the authority of the blood of Jesus, exercising authority over the external onslaught of the enemy. When you are confronted with the wrong attitudes of others, always ask the Lord to examine your heart to see if you are guilty of the same attitude. The reason for examining your heart is this challenge: "How can you take authority over something that you are also guilty of?"

"And why worry about a speck in your friend's eye when you have a log in your own? How can you think of saying, 'Let me

help you get rid of the speck in your eye' when you can't see
past the log in your own eye?"   *Matthew 7:3-4 (NLT)*

Submitting a Prophetic Word

The proper attitude in giving a prophetic word is to submit it with a humble heart. Humility is vital for the word to be received properly. If you have an abrasive attitude, your pastor can discern the spirit in which a word is delivered. An angry, arrogant, or manipulative spirit does not reflect the Spirit of God. A pastor may dismiss a prophetic word simply because of the attitude in which it was given.

After a prophetic word is submitted, trust the Lord to confirm the word. If a pastor takes action on a prophecy, it always should be because there is a confirmation in his own spirit. Never badger or try to force an agreement of the prophetic word. If any revelation really is from God, the Lord will be faithful to confirm the word. Your pastor needs the freedom to judge the word, discern the timing, and to even not confirm it.

Be careful not to assume that a pastor's lack of response is an indicator that he is not hearing from God. From a leader's point of view, there may be a timing issue involved or he may not bear witness with the word. It is important to understand that after you submit a prophetic word to leadership, it is no longer your responsibility. The accountability for a submitted word is between the Lord and the pastor.

I have heard horror stories of prophetic intercessors calling pastors in the middle of the night because they received a prophecy that just could not wait until morning. I have heard other stories of pastors being threatened that, if they did not heed a particular prophecy, the Lord would shut down their church. This behavior is manipulative, controlling, and completely out of order. It also does not reflect the Spirit of the Lord.

Charismatic Witchcraft

Be careful not to pray prayers that are a manipulative exercise of your will over a person's life or situation. Manipulative prayers are a form of witchcraft that negatively influences a person's life and even becomes a form of harassment. Witchcraft is when someone accesses or invokes a power outside the Spirit of God. By praying prayers that are outside of the will of God, spoken words can become demonically charged. Witchcraft occurs when a demonic power attaches itself to a thought or a spoken word. When you pray outside the will of God, the person you are praying for may experience harassing thoughts trying to influence them in a certain direction.

Several years ago, this happened to me. A married couple, who I did not know very well, decided to pray that I would marry a particular man. Their prayers were done without my knowledge or agreement. However, I felt the effect of their prayers. This couple's persistent prayers manifested in my life as harassing thoughts. For two years, I had thoughts that I should marry this man, even though I was not attracted to him. No matter how hard I tried, I just couldn't seem to shake the thoughts bombarding my mind. At one point, I actually felt guilty that I did not have any romantic feelings for him. Every time I was around this man, it reminded me of the unnatural pressure I felt to marry him. So, then I began to avoid him. What irritated me the most was how I felt my will was somehow violated as I tried to resist these thoughts and I did not know why. The harassing thoughts did not end until finally it was revealed how this couple had been praying and were asked to stop. I felt the effects immediately! This is why it is important to pray the Lord's will and not your own. If you are not sure how to pray about a matter, you can always ask the Lord for direction or pray in tongues.

"Likewise the Spirit also helps us in our weaknesses. For we do not know what we should prayer for as we ought, but the Spirit Himself makes intercession for us through groanings which cannot be uttered."   Romans 8:16 (NLT)

Aligning With the Church Vision

Remember that the senior pastor is the person God uses to establish the church vision and direction. Why? Because the pastor is the one chosen by the Lord to lead the local church body.

What would happen if all the sheep started to do their own thing and not follow the leading of the shepherd? For one thing, there would be no protection, unity, or a way for the body to function together. Instead, there would be anarchy and confusion. Our job as intercessors is to undergird and support the vision set forth by the leadership.

So why does it sometimes seem that prophetic intercessors can see what is coming before the pastor does? If you are called as a prophetic intercessor or a watchman who prays for the church, remember the vision and direction already has been set in motion by the leadership. What you see prophetically should be in line with the course already in place.

Picture with me, for a moment, the lines on a highway. As you drive along and depending on the weather conditions, you often can see a fair distance ahead of you. As you travel down a stretch of highway, you have the vantage point to see what is coming. It is important to understand that if you were not on that particular route you would not see those things.

Having a particular vantage point is also true with the church vision and your role as a prophetic intercessor. You are being given insight based on the direction or the route God has already given to the pastor.

Sometimes even pastors have misunderstood why prophetic intercessors receive strong revelation and the pastors feel threatened. Feeling threatened is justified when intercessors are acting out of order and not walking in proper submission. On the other hand, sometimes pastors have wondered, "Why are these intercessors receiving revelation similar to what I receive in leading the church?" Some pastors have reacted to an intercessor's revelation with suspicion and perceived it as an attempt to usurp authority.

What pastors need to understand is why some intercessors are so prophetically aware. God has called intercessors to walk closely to Him as they carry His heart in praying for the church. They not only pray for God's favor and blessing, but they also discern any demonic hindrances that would oppose the leadership in implementing the vision. The role of a prophetic intercessor is to watch and pray. In prayer they are like the Special Forces the military uses to carry out secret missions. The secret missions of God are designed to weaken the enemy's defenses and allow for a greater advance.

Any prophetic revelation that intercessors receive is given by God to support the leadership and protect the work of God. Because of the prophetic nature of some intercessors, often they discern strategies that will help the church to advance. For this reason, a clear communication flow between the pastor and a prophetic intercessory team is essential.

Communication Flow

Each church, depending on the size of the congregation, has its own pattern of prayer and communication between intercessors and the church leadership. Some churches have a prayer pastor, a prayer coordinator, or head intercessor overseeing the prayer ministries. Because each church is unique, I would like to share some general suggestions that you can adapt to meet the needs of your church.

Consider for a moment, a hypothetical situation. Picture a church where the prophetic intercessory team meets every two weeks with either a prayer pastor or prayer coordinator reporting directly to the senior pastor. The team's prayer assignment is to pray protection over the vision of the church. Given this scenario, let us take a look at what a healthy connection should look like.

One of the first things that should be established is a liaison person to meet with the pastor regularly to share what is being discerned during the prophetic prayer meetings. Usually the liaison is the team leader. If the prayer pastor is not the leader, then the team leader should keep the prayer pastor updated on any significant revelation to pass on to the senior pastor. For this situation, assume that the prayer pastor is leading the team.

Monthly Meetings

A regularly scheduled monthly meeting between the liaison and the senior pastor an effective way to establish a solid connection with the intercessors. The meeting is an opportunity for the senior pastor to be updated on any current prophetic theme and for the prophetic intercessors to be given feedback. It is also a chance for the senior pastor to share upcoming church events that need prayer coverage, discuss and plan prayer initiatives or how to further develop the prayer ministry within the church. This meeting time also allows the liaison to communicate more freely than in a written report. For the prayer team, a regular meeting helps to establish a feeling of connectedness, purpose, and an affirmation that the team's prayers are significant and appreciated. In addition to the monthly meetings, it is valuable for the senior pastor to attend the prophetic prayer meetings every so often, even if only for a short time. The trust level and accountability that is built through these connecting points are invaluable to growth of the team as well as communicating a validation of the prophetic intercessory team.

Report Writing

Another important connecting point is a regular written report to the senior pastor or to whomever the prophetic team reports to[68]. This report should be written regularly and serves as a valuable accountability tool. My suggestion is to write a report monthly. If the prayer meeting is every two weeks, then the report should be written after each prayer meeting. This report can be flexible depending on your relationship with the senior pastor. If writing a report is not possible because of time constraints, then verbal communication is a good way to give a

---

[68] Prayer Pastor or Prayer Coordinator

brief update. A report should include a general update on what is being discerned prophetically as well as how the team is doing.

Usually I follow a certain criterion for these kinds of updates. If the pastor was not in the meeting, my job is to communicate just enough information to give the pastor a clear sense of what happened, but not overwhelm him with unnecessary details. So I begin by asking myself the question, "What would be helpful for the leadership to know?"

As a general practice, I have someone on the team write down any prophetic revelation received during our prayer times. This person is our so-called *scribe*. We keep this information in a notebook so I can later refer to it when updating our pastor. The first step in writing a report is to ask the Holy Spirit to guide me as I write. Then, I use a highlighting pen to highlight the major prophetic themes recorded during the meeting.

Writing a report like this can feel overwhelming. Usually I read through about fifteen pages of notes filled with all the details of the prophetic flow for that evening. I have learned to look for the 'prophetic thread' in the meeting. In other words, I try to identify the major themes that the Lord was revealing to us that evening. It is important to remember that your pastor does not need a lot of detail to catch the general sense of the prophetic flow. It is helpful to highlight key words and phrases. Then, it is just a matter of adding enough details to bring clarity to what's communicated.

Intercessors often wrestle with a temptation to share all the details of their prophetic revelation with others. Many times they make no attempt to connect their insight to how the Lord has been speaking to the church already or to relate it to the prophetic season the church is in. This lack of connection makes it difficult for the person listening to understand the prophetic significance of the revelation and how it relates to the current season. It is important for intercessors to learn how to recognize and articulate the prophetic thread (or the main point) of what the Lord is saying. It is like writing a story summary. In a summary not all the details are necessary to communicate the essence of the story. The ability to summarize the prophetic themes is an important skill in communicating prophetic revelation to church leadership.

During a prayer meeting there are usually two or three prophetic threads that are important to share with the leadership. Many times, as I write reports, the Lord will give me further revelation that enables me to clearly communicate the prophetic revelation the team discerned.

I do pay careful attention to how a report appears visually. If you send a report with long paragraphs or no paragraph breaks, it can appear visually overwhelming to the reader. It does not inspire someone to take the time to read it. Remember, pastors are busy people with limited time. If you set a pattern of writing long reports, the pastor may to put your report in the backlog of things to do when there is more time.

The key is to write concisely, organize the information so that it is not visually overwhelming, and discern what revelation would be important to share with the leadership. If I find that just one prayer point needs more than a page and a half, then I send a second e-mail. I never try to cram a long report all into one. Two short e-mails are easier to digest than one long one!

Here are some guidelines to make a report appear more bite-sized:

- Keep the report no longer than a page and a half.

- Make paragraph breaks after every three or four lines.

- Organize the report by category (for example, church body or a particular event).

- Communicate the prophetic threads and leave out any unnecessary details.

- Be sure to add just enough detail for the context of the revelation to be clear.

- Connect the revelation to what God is already speaking to the congregation or the prophetic season of the church.

When should a report be written? Generally within the week, or no later than two weeks, after the prayer meeting and definitely before the next meeting. If you wait too long, it is more difficult to remember the prophetic sense or relevancy of what was discerned.

Once the Report is Sent, Now What?

After the report is written and submitted to the pastor, he will need time to process this information and respond with feedback. One of the things I appreciate about our pastor is how he handles these reports! He will usually read it through quickly and send me a quick e-mail with an initial response. Because of the prophetic nature of what is written, our pastor often will take time later to read and pray through it during his devotional time. Reading and praying about the report gives him an opportunity to discern the mind of the Lord about the revelation as well as any follow-through that is needed. This is an excellent example of how prophetic intercessors can partner together with church leadership.

It is important to understand that after we submit a prophetic word, it becomes the responsibility of leadership to seek the Lord's wisdom concerning that Word. We need to trust our leaders to seek God in how they are to respond or implement any prophetic revelation. We must never place our personal feeling of validation on whether or not a word is received. It is a major pitfall to avoid! Our only responsibility is to be good stewards of what we believe God has given to us prophetically. We can trust if we have heard correctly that the Lord will be faithful to confirm his word.

When to Approach Leadership with Revelation

If you are on a prophetic intercession team and you receive a prophetic word other than during the prayer meeting, it is a good idea to present the word to the team leader before submitting it to the pastor. There are times when this is not necessary. For example, if you are in a corporate prayer setting and the pastor asks if anyone has a prophetic sense, then by all means share it! What we want to avoid is a steady stream of intercessors all wanting to share their prophetic words with the pastor. This is why it is helpful to submit prophetic words through the leaders of the prayer ministry.

Sometimes you can catch a pastor right after a church service if you really sense that you are supposed to speak to him personally. However, be sensitive when you approach during this time because your pastor may need to be focusing on connecting with new converts, new people visiting the church, prayer for those who are hurting, or hosting a guest speaker. Just know that if you are really supposed to share a prophetic word that the Lord will open up the right opportunity!

What are the benefits of a prophetic intercessor aligning with their pastor?

What are the benefits when prophetic intercessors align with their pastors? Although we will discuss these benefits in Chapter 11, I would like to briefly touch on a few things. The first and foremost reason for right alignment is that it is by

God's design[69]. We are all called to function in our unique roles in the body of Christ. For each part to add strength to the whole, we need to be willing to receive each other.

Some people are called to be pastors[70]. The benefit of this role in the body of Christ has to do with the rich deposit God has given that leader. Pastors have a special grace God has designed to strengthen the church. In scripture, the chief role of a shepherd is to be protective[71]. The Lord has equipped pastors with a sensitivity to certain dangers that will harm the sheep or lead them astray. Pastors provide protection and spiritual covering to those under their care. As they lead, they have learned how to gently guide others in the ways of godliness and even assist in the healing process when there has been injury.

The pastoral leadership team can communicate the word of God so that it becomes spiritual food to strengthen others. Some strengthening has to do with character building and helping others to see their blind spots. Pastoral oversight works to bring health and wholeness to the congregation. As part of the fivefold ministry, pastors are called by God to raise up the body of Christ to do the work of the ministry.

For prophetic intercessors to function properly, they must be willing to receive the care and oversight of a shepherd. The wisdom, guidance, and spiritual foundation that this relationship

---

[69] Jeremiah 3:15
[70] Ephesians 4:11
[71] John 10:11

provides is vital to keeping one's character and anointing in balance. One of my pastors once said, "What your anointing or spiritual gifting will build up, your undeveloped character will tear down." Unfortunately, too often we have seen this principle in action. Many in the church have fallen because their character has not developed in parallel with their spiritual gift or calling.

If your experience with church leadership and pastors has been a difficult one, let me take this opportunity as a pastor to ask for your forgiveness on behalf of those leaders. God's intention is for you is to be in a place of health and protection. If you are not, my exhortation to you is to forgive those who, in their humanity, have been a source of hurt and pain for you. Then, seek the Lord's wisdom about what he is requiring you to do. God may call you to another church. Just be careful not assign blame to your leadership for issues God is really trying to deal with in you. It is very important to seek the wisdom of the Lord and the counsel of other mature Christians and spiritual leaders in discerning the Lord's direction.

In Conclusion

Keeping in proper alignment to church leadership is foundational to the proper operation of any prophetic intercession team. It has all to do with God's divine order of things for His church. Having a clear view of our position in Christ, right attitudes, and pastoral and intercessory roles are essential in order to effectively co-labor. When these principles are clearly understood and embraced, health comes to the body of Christ in the proper functioning of our respective ministry roles. God also takes great delight in this right relationship because of the way it strengthens the body as a whole!

"And He Himself gave some to be apostles, some prophets, some evangelists, some pastors, and teachers, for the equipping of the saints for the work of the ministry, for the edifying of the body of Christ, till we all come to the unity of the faith and the knowledge of the Son of God, to a perfect man, to the measure of the stature of the fullness of Christ; that we should no longer be children, tossed to and fro and carried about with every wind of doctrine, by the trickery of men, in the cunning craftiness of deceitful plotting, but, speaking the truth in love, may grow up in all things into Him who is the head— Christ—from whom the whole body, joined and knit together by what every joint supplies, according to the effective working by which every part does its share, causes growth of the body for the edifying of itself in love."   Ephesians 4:10-16

A Word to Pastors and Prophetic Intercessors

"Consider what I say, and may the Lord give you understanding in all things."   2 Timothy 2:7

As the importance of prophetic intercession continues to emerge in the body of Christ, I would like to address some common misunderstandings and misperceptions between pastors and prophetic intercessors. Most of these problems come from pastors and intercessors not understanding how the other person thinks or how they are called to relate to one another. Intercessors are often characterized as unusual people—especially if they operate in some of the spiritual gifts listed in I Corinthians 12:7-12: word of knowledge, word of wisdom, discernment of spirits, and prophecy. If you are a pastor who does not function in the prophetic, has had difficult experiences with intercessors, or just does not feel you can relate to prophetic intercessory-type people, I have a few thoughts to share with you about some misunderstandings. Even if you personally have not had difficulty with prophetic intercessors, some of your praying people may be coming from churches where false perceptions have caused a lot of hurts and wounds. If you are a prophetic intercessor reading this book, I would like to discuss some of the potential challenges you may face in connecting with church leadership. My intention in addressing these issues is to facilitate understanding between pastors and intercessors so they can move into a place of healthy interaction in their respective roles.

Prophetic Intercessors and Pastors Need Each Other

As we have discussed, for prophetic intercessors to fully function in their intercessory role, a healthy connection to the leadership must be established and maintained. Pastors, the fact that intercessors have been placed under your care is the first sign that you are called to play a significant role in the development of their spiritual growth and maturity. Many times prophetic intercessors appear *strange* because they are not properly relating to pastoral authority, or grounded in the Word, or properly processing the prophetic insight they receive. A lack in any of these areas can cause intercessors to be biblically off-track by becoming secretive, esoteric, and critical of leadership. Intercessors need to remember that what they discern prophetically needs to line up with the Word of God and to align with the direction that the leadership has set. It is so important for prophetic intercessors to be willing to receive instruction and correction from pastors, regardless of whether intercessors feel that their intercessory gift is understood. This leads me to the first of several areas of misunderstanding between pastors and intercessors.

The following are some common perceptions, held by either prophetic intercessors or church leaders, that have caused misunderstanding in the body of Christ.

Perception #1: My pastor does not understand my prophetic-intercessory gift.

This perception may or may not be true, but the perception is potentially dangerous and is often the culprit in causing intercessors to not align properly with leadership. One sign of this problem is an unwillingness to receive counsel from leadership. There are several reasons why an intercessor might be unwilling to receive counsel and it is worthwhile to take a closer look at some of those reasons.

Some intercessors may feel misunderstood because of previous experiences that have nothing to do with their current pastor. When there has been a previous offense, misunderstanding, or even a mishandling of an intercessor, patience is needed while the process of healing occurs and trust is rebuilt. When a person refuses to receive instruction from a leader, usually there is emotional pain and a breach of trust involved. Unfortunately, as a spiritual leader, you may be reaping the repercussions of another leader's poor relational interaction. Even before you can speak to a person's pain, you must build a foundation of unconditional love and affirmation to prepare for a receptive heart, that is unless someone asks you to speak into their life or their behavior warrants a confrontation. If you are the spiritual leader who has caused the offense, it is so important to humble yourself, ask for forgiveness, and look for ways to rebuild a healthy connection.

As spiritual leaders, it is very humbling to admit when we have been wrong, especially when most of our life is given in the service of helping others. Yet, we sometimes think that it compromises our ability to lead if we ever appear wrong. On the contrary, a strong leader should be a person who can easily humble himself or herself and admit a mistake. Unfortunately, many leaders are afraid to be transparent. Instead, they ignore their mistakes, in hopes that the issues will magically disappear, and then continue on without ever making their mistakes right. Failing to acknowledge and deal with mistakes not only undermines a leader's credibility, it also reveals a heart that is not right.

The challenge is the same for intercessors. We must be willing to acknowledge and repent of wrong heart attitudes, especially in our judgment of church leadership. Although all of us are responsible before God to release forgiveness towards one another, the Bible also warns us to be careful to not become a stumbling block to others because of our actions.

"It is good neither to eat meat nor drink wine nor do anything by which your brother stumbles or is offended or is made weak."

Romans 14:21

Another reason an intercessor may be resistant to church leadership is from a lack of instruction on how to properly relate to leadership. In this case, foundational teaching is needed. Believe it or not, lack of training happens a lot more than we realize. As leaders, we mistakenly make an assumption that intercessors should know better. Intercessors are also guilty in assuming that pastors should automatically understand how to relate to intercessors. God still is bringing clarity to the body of Christ about prayer and how intercessors are to partner with leadership. For this reason, it is logical that there is still misunderstanding and confusion about this issue. Just because intercessors do not understand how to properly relate to leadership does not make them guilty of intentionally undermining authority. The same is true for the pastor who struggles in connecting with intercessors. The pastor should not be characterized as uncaring or unspiritual due to a lack of understanding.

Currently there are different perspectives between pastors and intercessors about the role that prayer and intercession should play in the local church. These differences have to do with church size, styles, personal preferences, and personal views of the place prayer and intercession should have in the local church. Churches are at different stages of how prayer is valued and implemented. Regardless of how prayer is viewed, senior pastors are still the ones to bring clarity about how prayer is expressed in their particular church.

We always must remember that God has entrusted pastors to watch over the lives of the people in their congregations.

Sometimes when pastors are not familiar with intercessors and are unsure of how to encourage them in their spiritual gifts, they inadvertently distance themselves. Distancing is often interpreted as rejection and opens a door for the intercessors to feel isolated, misunderstood, and rejected.

If you are a leader who is uncomfortable with intercessors, be careful how you express this uneasiness. Some pastors have made casual remarks from the pulpit, in attempts to be funny, on how weird and strange intercessors seem to be. Just because someone has a different expression in their spiritual gift does not make them weird. Insensitive remarks only serve to create an atmosphere of disrespect toward intercessors in the way they are viewed by others in the church. Insensitive remarks do not communicate an honoring or a valuing of intercessors as a necessary part of the body of Christ.

From an intercessor's standpoint, being characterized as weird or strange may even cause the intercessor to feel ashamed and devalued. The intercessor may take offense, especially when a leader has spoken unfairly. Most people view their pastors as a place of safety. When a person has felt dishonored or mistreated by church leadership, they no longer feel safe. Rather, they feel a violation of trust. Imagine how difficult it is for intercessors to be open to correction or instruction when a leader is speaking a negative view of intercessors or is avoiding them.

Whether or not you, as a spiritual leader, have been guilty of this kind of negative communication, understand many of your intercessors may have experienced dishonor in a previous church and are wondering if you will do the same. Painful experiences may be part of their hesitation in connecting with you. It is very beneficial to ask new people about their previous church experiences and the ministry experiences they have had.

Perception #2: My church does not believe prayer is connected to effective ministry.

When pastors do not recognize the necessity of prayer or intercession as one of the vital tools God has given the church to advance His kingdom purposes, several things may happen.

- A disconnection between pastors and intercessors will exist within the culture of that local church that can result in intercessors feeling isolated, alone, and unable to come into the fullness of their intercessory call.

- The leadership may experience more difficulty in moving forward in the overall church vision, not only because of the lack of prayer, but also because part of the body of Christ is not being used.

- Pastors become less effective as leaders.

Why is this true? Because moving forward in effective ministry is rooted in prayer. Prayer is a place of dependency on God, in a personal and corporate sense. Prayer is where we can seek the Lord's wisdom and counsel for the challenges we encounter or the plans we desire to implement. We must remember that we live in a fallen world with an enemy who seeks to oppose the gospel of truth from going forth to lost and dying people.

There is a very strong picture in scripture connecting kingdom advancement with effectual, fervent prayer[72]. An example of effectual, fervent prayer occurred when Peter was unjustly imprisoned[73]. The church gathered to pray for his release. In response to these prayers, God sent an angel to miraculously deliver Peter from prison so that he could continue to lead the Church.

We need to be discerning the Lord's wisdom when faced with the enemy's opposition. This is where prayer and intercession are powerful weapons in resisting the enemy's schemes. What kind of spiritual opposition do we encounter? Mostly, it comes in the form of thoughts and lies that deceive our minds from discerning the truth, delays that are meant to discourage us, offenses that are aimed to divide the body of Christ, infirmity that weakens our physical body, and fears that try to paralyze us from moving forward. Why does the enemy resist the advance of the kingdom? It all has to do with the fulfillment of the Great Commission[74].

---

[72] James 5:16
[73] Acts 12:3-19
[74] Mark 16:15

The resistance we experience, as the church advances, is the reason that Jesus has taken a position of prayer before the Father, on our behalf[75]. The Bible declares that Jesus lives to make intercession so that His work on Earth will continue to grow. Intercessors are called by God to stand alongside leaders to *watch and pray* as a ministry moves forward. Prophetic intercessors can offer a unique insight in confirming and protecting the work of God. Many times God gives prophetic intercessors a specific strategy about how to pray to counter the schemes of the enemy. Intercessors also can discern how the spirit of God desires to move in a situation and pray in agreement. This prayer of agreement is a powerful tool in defeating the enemy's resistance.

I have known pastors who experienced a dramatic change in the effectiveness of their ministry when they mobilized intercessors to pray. I once knew a pastor who was heavily involved in street evangelism. Every week, for several years, he would take teams of people downtown to do street evangelism. They would pass out Bibles, share the gospel with whoever would listen, and they experienced a measure of success. Although this pastor prayed for God to bless his efforts, he did not have a team of intercessors praying regularly for this ministry.

Then one year the area churches began to join together in reaching the lost people of the city. As the regional intercessors

---

[75] Hebrews 7:25

began to connect and include this pastor in their prayers, he began to experience a dramatic change in the effectiveness of his ministry. He noticed that people on the street were more open to the gospel and found the workers were passing out more Bibles in one week than over a couple of months. The pastor wondered what was causing this change. Finally, it occurred to him that it had to be the united prayer of the churches. Up to that point, he had never seen the connection between committed prayer and effective ministry.

Increasing the effectiveness of ministry is one reason why it is helpful for pastors to intentionally establish a connection with intercessors or intercessory groups in their church. This connection, admittedly, may take them beyond their comfort level. Pastors, I encourage you to be willing to spend a little time in prayer with your intercessors and learn how another part of the body of Christ functions. When you pray together, intercessors and pastors can learn to value each other as a vital part of the body of Christ. As in marriage, the distinct differences strengthen us as we learn to appreciate one another. Both pastors and intercessors need to be willing to learn from each other, especially because their partnership impacts the advance of kingdom purposes.

Perception #3: Intercessors are strange people and appear super-spiritual.

When we talk about intercessors who are behaving strangely or who appear to be super-spiritual, we are referring to intercessors who are doing things to an excessive degree or outside the accepted cultural norm. Before we continue, it is important to note that the Bible is full of examples of signs, wonders, and miracles that could easily fit this description according to societal norms. For example, the prophet Ezekiel was instructed by God to lie on his left side for 390 days as a sign to the house of Israel about the siege God was sending against Jerusalem[76]. There is no question that Ezekiel's actions appeared very odd to the people of his day. Jesus himself healed a man of blindness by spitting on the ground and making a paste that he placed over the eyes of this man, and then told him to go wash in the pool of Siloam[77]. Again, to the people of Jesus' day, this did not fit the societal norm.

I certainly would not advocate people justifying weird behavior just because unusual incidents have been recorded in the Bible. However, we do need to remember that the Spirit of God often transcends our human understanding of reality. For example, we understand sickness to be a natural part of our human condition. Yet, sickness and death were unknown to Adam and Eve in the Garden of Eden. It was not natural to them. Sickness and death only became a physical reality after sin was introduced into the world. In the miracles Jesus performed in the New Testament, he paints a contrasting picture of this spiritual truth. He shows us that although sickness and disease are a part of our natural existence, we

---

[76] Ezekiel 4:3-8
[77] John 9:1-7

can also experience healing and deliverance through the power of the Holy Spirit. From the miracles that Jesus performed, we can see how the Spirit of God is not limited to any natural law that defines our earthly existence. His miracle working power transcends this reality.

With this principle in mind, whenever we observe strange or unusual behavior we should ask if it is inspired by the Spirit of God. The following are some suggested indicators in determining whether a person's behavior or prophetic revelation is of God.

Indicator #1: Does it line up with the Word of God?

When intercessors are not grounded in the Word of God nor allow the prophetic words or discernment to be judged or tested scripturally, there is a danger of being deceived. Keep in mind that some revelations cannot be found in scripture in a literal sense, but can be seen in principle or as a pattern in scripture. For example, we know from the Bible that God can speak through dreams and visions. In the book of Genesis we understand through the life of Joseph that God reveals the symbolic language of dreams.

When Joseph was brought before the ruler of Egypt, Pharaoh said, *"I had a dream and there is no one who can interpret it. But I have heard it said of you that you can understand a dream, to interpret it."* Genesis 41:15a (NKJV)

Joseph's response is crucial. He told Pharaoh, *"It is not me; God will give Pharaoh an answer of peace."*

Genesis 41:16 (NKJV)

The Bible is clear that God is the interpreter of dreams and our understanding of a dream should also line up with biblical patterns. That is why it is important to train intercessors to use the Word of God as their spiritual compass to guide them in their prophetic expression. It is especially helpful to have an intercessory leader who is mature in the Word and can discern when a prophetic sensing is demonic, soulish, biblically off-track, or anointed of God.

Indicator #2: Is the behavior or prophetic word inspired by the Holy Spirit?

Sometimes what begins in the Spirit ends up in the flesh[78]. Just because something starts with the earmarks of the Holy Spirit does not guarantee all of it is divinely inspired. It is important to look for spiritual fruit as well as to discern the spirit of a person's words or actions. Some important questions to ask are these.

- Do you sense a wrong spirit (division, rebellion, manipulation, pride, control, or anger) surrounding what is being done or spoken? Or do you see the fruit of the spirit: love, peace, joy, patience, self-control, faith, and meekness as the characterizing nature?

---

[78] Galatians 3:3

- Is the nature of God clearly discernable and consistent with His character biblically? People can be sincerely deceived due to blind spots in their own character or in their understanding of the scriptures. Blind spots can taint how they view what they think they are receiving prophetically because they are adding their own understanding to interpret what they sense.

- Who is glorified in this behavior or prophetic revelation? God, man, or the devil?

- Is the behavior soulish in nature?

- Is this person a mature believer, grounded in the Word of God, and submitted to leadership?

Indicator #3: Are there occult or cult-like overtones?

Accessing secret knowledge or power other than through the Holy Spirit is a violation of scripture. Therefore, consulting with angels, demons or spirit guides, participating in séances, reading tarot cards, palm reading, seeking the counsel of a medium, and casting spells are all a counterfeit means of accessing spiritual knowledge and power. Even praying according to your will and not God's will can be a subtle form of witchcraft because of the control and manipulation involved. Also, watch out for anything that appears secretive or causes people to separate themselves from the body of Christ because of the special revelation that they claim God has given to them. Other questions to consider include these.

- Is there exclusiveness to the revelation?

- What is the attitude of the person toward other believers or leadership?

- Is the person teachable, humble, and open to correction? Or does the person become defensive and critical when challenged?

These are important indicators that something may be out of order.

Indicator #4: Do you have a sense of confirmation with the behavior in your spirit?

In judging a prophetic word or discerning unusual behavior, a critical question is this, "Do you have a witness in your spirit or are you uneasy?"

Uneasiness or a lack of peace is a red flag to pay attention to. You may need to spend time in prayer to determine why you feel uncomfortable. You may also need to speak with the person involved in more depth to gain the necessary clarity. We also need to separate a prophetic word from the messenger. It is great when a person's attitude matches the prophetic message they deliver, but it is not always the case. Sometimes there is a mix where the revelation is correct, but the person's attitude needs adjusting. On the other hand, sometimes a person's negative demeanor can be a red flag that the revelation is not from God.

Indicator #5: Is it occurring in proper proportion to how it occurs in the Bible?

In other words, how often does the behavior or prophetic revelation occur in scripture? For example, sometimes prophetic intercessors can mistake their own human understanding as a prompting of the Holy Spirit to perform a prophetic act. It happens when they begin to turn every prophetic insight into a prophetic act. Just because you can imagine a prophetic act does not mean that the Holy Spirit is prompting you to do one. We must discern, "Is God is truly prompting us, or it is just a nice idea?"

When we measure how often prophetic acts occur in scripture, we find that they were not a common experience. In fact, prophetic acts were rare. I believe God intended prophetic acts to be that way. It is like using exclamation points in punctuation. Exclamation points are intended to show strong feeling as a form of emphasis. If every sentence ended in an exclamation point, we would not regard this punctuation as special or something to pay particular attention to. It would become ordinary. The same is true with prophetic acts. Because of the rare use in scripture, when a prophetic act does occur, it is intended to be a special emphasis that draws our attention to what God is revealing.

Perception #4: Intercessors talk in a way I cannot relate to.

Prophetic intercessors do seem to have a language all their own. Because of their prophetic gift, intercessors see life differently from other people. Because of their perceptions, sometimes intercessors have over-spiritualized natural life experiences by looking for the spiritual significance in everything that happens.

For example, just because someone has a flat tire does not mean he or she is under spiritual attack. A flat tire is a common experience in life. However, a flat tire can be a form of spiritual attack when several disruptive events happen in a short period of time. Let's say one morning you lose your wallet, your car stalls, you cannot find an important file at work, you struggle to concentrate, and are interrupted constantly. When these events are not normal and you are tempted to feel frustrated or discouraged, it could be that a hindering spirit is buffeting you.

Should we interpret life events as spiritual attack every time things go wrong? No, but sometimes there is a spiritual aspect to our everyday difficulties. Prophetic intercessors have spiritual gifts that enable them to discern spiritual activity. However, intercessors do need to be careful to be prompted by the Holy Spirit when they attach spiritual meaning to natural events.

Pastors, especially those who struggle to relate to prophetic intercessors, should be careful not to dismiss the spiritual perspective of a situation too quickly. There may be some spiritual activity going on that you need to consider. It is devaluing to intercessors to be characterized as being so super-spiritual that what they say is considered invalid. Prophetic intercessors often see life through a different perspective and may discern things that others have not. This does not mean intercessors are more spiritual than others. Rather, intercessors are positioned by God to support pastors. Prophetic gifts are designed by God to strengthen and protect the body of Christ.

Another thing that can make it difficult to relate to prophetic intercessors is the way they convey a prophetic revelation. For intercessors, trying to formulate words to describe what they spiritually discern is like trying to describe an abstract painting. Intercessors learn to recognize patterns in what they prophetically see, and then try to use familiar words to communicate it. At times, intercessors use proper names in referring to a demonic spirit such as Jezebel or Leviathan. These are biblical names used to symbolize demonic characteristics. For example, Jezebel is described in the Bible as an evil queen who was known for being manipulative, controlling, and seductive[79]. So if prophetic intercessors say that they discern a Jezebel spirit, they mean they are

---

[79] 1 Kings 21:1-29

discerning a spirit with these characteristics. Leviathan is another biblical term used in referring to the sin of Lucifer—pride[80]. Proper names are often used by intercessors to express the functional features of a demonic spirit.

Many times God communicates a prophetic message in the form of pictures (visions and dreams) that intercessors attempt to describe. There is a great example in Ezekiel of the prophet describing the unusual things he saw in a vision.

"Now as I looked at the living creatures, behold a wheel was on the earth beside each living creature with its four faces. The appearance of the wheels and their workings was like the color of beryl, and all four had the same likeness. The appearance of their workings was, as it were, a wheel in the middle of a wheel." Ezekiel 1:15-16

Sometimes it is hard to describe prophetic pictures or images that are unfamiliar, so like Ezekiel, we make sense of them by describing the images with familiar objects. With these visions often comes an instant understanding of what the Lord is speaking. It is not unusual for prophetic intercessors to share a vision, dream, impression, or discernment with the same kind of descriptive imagery found in Ezekiel. Personally I encourage prophetic intercessors to communicate this kind of prophetic revelation in relatable terms. Instead of sharing all the imagery, just simply convey the interpretation.

---

[80] Isaiah 14:13-15

It is also helpful to use the functional names of demonic spirits in sharing spiritual discernment to others. For example, instead of using a proper name like Rahab, use the functional name which is chaos and confusion. Everyone can relate to times when things are chaotic or confusing, instead of calling it a Rahab spirit[81]. Unless the person you are speaking to is familiar with this language, they will not know what you are referring to.

Perception #5: There are no differences among intercessors in their prayer expression or calling.

Sometimes people assume that, because someone has an intercessory call, he or she desires to pray for any and all prayer requests. Among intercessors there are different types of prayer burdens, spiritual gifts, and intercessory callings that distinguish one intercessor from another.

One difference relates to prayer burdens. Prayer burdens are God-inspired prayer assignments that an intercessor feels a special desire to pray about. For example, God might give you a burden to pray for children and youth, church leaders, missionaries, a geographical area or neighborhood, local or state government, emergency prayer requests, and so on. Many intercessors have several prayer burdens and participate on several prayer teams. Some of these prayer assignments are short-term while others are long-lasting.

---

[81] Isaiah 51:9; Job 26:12

Another distinction is between intercessors who are prophetic in their intercessory expression and those who are not. The main difference is how the prophetic gifts are activated during prayer[82]. Understanding this difference is an important point to consider when organizing corporate prayer meetings.

General intercessors typically receive a burden from God to pray, but they do not flow consistently in the prophetic gifts as part of their intercessory expression. Many of these prayer warriors enjoy praying over lists of things and usually move quickly from one prayer focus to another as they feel led. Then there are prophetic intercessors. Prophetic intercessors function strongly in one or more of the prophetic gifts[83]. Their prayer pattern is to focus on one prayer point for a while before moving onto the next. This happens because, as they wait upon the Lord, the prophetic gifts are activated. Prophetic gifts give insight into the direction the Lord wants the person to pray. Both kinds of intercessory expressions are needed to keep the body of Christ covered in prayer.

The last difference has to do with different types of intercessory callings, such as the call to be a watchman or personal intercessor. My intercessory call is to be a watchman for both the local and regional church and occasionally for nations as well. Because of my call, I have an ongoing sense of the spiritual climate of each area, much-like a personal intercessor

---

[82] Reference Chapter 3
[83] Reference Chapter 2

has a continual burden to pray for a particular person or spiritual leader.

As you can see, there are several unique distinctions about an intercessor's call to prayer. Intercessors certainly can pray for various areas of need, but we should respect the fact that most intercessors feel called to intercede about certain things and be careful not to overwhelm them with other prayer requests. The truth is ALL Christians are called to pray. The responsibility of praying has not been given to intercessors alone[84].

Perception #6: Intercessors appear to be ultra sensitive and emotional

This is a common perception about intercessors who function strongly in the gift of the discernment of spirits. It is important to understand how a prophetic intercessor experiences life as a result of having this spiritual gift. The discernment of spirits involves a heightened awareness of the spiritual climate with the five senses sharpened to help the person in identifying the spiritual activity they discern. This type of spiritual sensing does not come and go like other prophetic expressions. For intercessors who have this gift, discernment never really shuts off. At least for me it does not. Over the years, other intercessors have reported the same. At times, I have wished the discernment would shut off!

---

[84] 1 Timothy 2:1-2

Although the gift causes a heightened ability to discern the spiritual atmosphere, it does not mean that the person is always focused on what he or she is discerning. In fact, sometimes I do not always catch the fact that I am discerning something and think it is just me. I really have had to learn how to separate what I spiritually discern from what I feel emotionally. There is a fine line between discernment and emotions. Be aware that discernment has to do with what God wants to reveal. Let me also make it clear that I do not have x-ray vision to see everyone's faults or shortcomings. However, sometimes God does reveal to me a person's problem area for the purpose of prayer.

Intercessors who have the gift of discernment tend to perceive conversations, words, and actions through their spiritual discernment. The challenge for them is they not only listen to what a person says, but also discern the spirit and motivation behind those words. Their spiritual gift gives them a greater sensitivity to know when something spoken is demonic, soulish, or carries the presence of God. When someone is speaking with a wrong motivation, often discerning intercessors can sense this motivation and, unfortunately, sometimes react poorly to it. Intercessors who react poorly to people need to grow in maturity.

All of us have a level of discernment that God gives us to distinguish right from wrong and to exercise wisdom in daily situations. Someone who has the gift of discernment has a heightened or sharper awareness. It is like a group of people standing twenty feet across the room from a painting. Although every one is standing approximately the same distance away and can see the same painting, the person with spiritual discernment might perceive the painting from two feet way rather than twenty. It is obvious there is a dramatic difference in perspective when you are viewing something twenty feet away compared to two feet. At two feet, the details are clearer and the painting takes up more of the field of vision. Accordingly, what is spiritually discerned sometimes can be overwhelming. It is like looking at life through a magnifying glass. Viewing life with spiritual discernment has challenges that can make a person appear strange to other people or even overly sensitive. As intercessors with a gift of discernment are maturing, they have to learn how to balance what they perceive with how God wants them to respond to what He is revealing.

One of the weaknesses of this gift is the temptation to respond in fear. Because of the ability to perceive things closely, it may even appear that intercessors are making a bigger deal out of what they discern than necessary. Again, this comes from the clarity by which they can perceive. When we are tempted to fear, an understanding of our position in Christ is critical[85]. We must carry a strong conviction in our hearts that God can overcome anything we discern. This conviction is so vital in learning how to respond correctly. At times, facing our fears

---

[85] Reference Ephesians Chapter 2

can be a challenge because we are human and it is easy to react in the flesh. I know for myself that at times I can discern things so quickly that I find myself reacting rather than responding, especially when I think it involves a selfish motivation or a demonic spirit behind someone's words.

Is spiritual discernment ever wrong? Yes, for example, when we view things through our emotional hurts or wounds, it skews our perception. As mentioned, fear is one thing that can throw us off balance as well as un-repented sin and pride. Also, not being firmly grounded in the Word can open a person to deception and false teaching, as we have seen at different times in the body of Christ. These are some of the pitfalls. It is helpful to have a mature circle of friends and a spiritual leader to process the challenges we encounter. Remaining in balance includes surrounding our lives with people we trust, are accountable to, and who can speak godly wisdom and counsel into our lives.

Relational issues also can be a challenge for discerning intercessors and for the pastors trying to guide them. Sometimes an intercessor reacts in fear and develops mistrust towards another person because of what he or she discerns about that person. It is especially hard when an intercessor discerns something of a demonic or manipulative nature that no one else seems to see. At such times, intercessors are tempted to feel isolated and mistrusting of people who may even be trying to help.

The key is to have the proper perspective in our response to any discernment that intercessors perceive. What is the proper response? God's heart is always to redeem and restore, which means that we should always take a posture of mercy and compassion when this discernment involves people. We need to be compassionate in how we treat someone even when we discern wrong attitudes or motives. One temptation is to move from discernment to being critical of a person, but this is not helpful. Our real warfare is against the demonic opposition in the spiritual realm, not people. However, that does not excuse a person from making poor choices or nullify our responsibility to confront a brother in love as Matthew 18 exhorts. We just need to pay attention to the spiritual aspect of what may be influencing a person, so that we can pray effectively.

The ability for an intercessor to discern spiritual activity often causes him or her to become a target of spiritual attack because the enemy does not want to be exposed. One form of attack is the schemes the enemy devises to discredit an intercessor. When an intercessor is spiritually attacked, she or he often can sense this happening in the circumstances around their life. This causes the person to feel afraid to share what she or he discerns. The fear is she or he will not be taken seriously or how the enemy twists situations or perceptions to look like the intercessor is the one at fault. It is another reason why sometimes intercessors feel very alone in what they discern.

For example, let's say that someone in the church is being influenced by a rebellious spirit and, unknown to the church leadership, is making comments that undermine spiritual authority. But because this person appears so charming and selfless in serving the church, the leadership has not discerned this wrong attitude or the subtle influence it is having. Suppose a prophetic intercessor named Anna discerns the deception around this spirit of rebellion and begins to feel very grieved. So Anna prays and begins to experience a lot of demonic opposition as she does. When she attempts to let church leadership know what she has discerned, Anna is told that she is being overly sensitive and critical. Anna walks away feeling devalued, misjudged, and grieved as she continues to discern the demonic activity. In the meantime, people are beginning to act disrespectfully and the leadership is puzzled about why this is happening. Unfortunately, this kind of scenario is not uncommon.

Now let's consider that Anna had been off in her discernment. It is certainly possible. In this situation the leadership needs to be discerning about the revelation that is submitted to them. The leadership needs to seek the Lord, especially if the revelation involves discernment about the motives of another person. The situation can cause great harm if the leaders act on a discernment that is inaccurate. More than she realizes, Anna may be viewing things from her own perspective and understanding. Could it be that Anna's past experiences and difficulties have colored her perception? Absolutely!

However, consider a word of caution. Just because someone has been through a difficult season does not necessarily invalidate what he or she perceives. In fact, a person may have a heightened spiritual sensitivity because of what he or she has been through. For example, I once knew a woman who dated a man who turned out to be very controlling and manipulative. Because of his charismatic personality, many people did not see this side of him. They just thought he was a lot of fun. Unfortunately, he had a pattern of dating women and speaking of a marriage commitment very early in the relationship. Then, he would suddenly end the relationship after a few months and move onto someone else. Unfortunately, this man lived by his emotions and was careless with his words. Truth for him one day was not truth for him the next because he lived by what he felt. The women he left behind were devastated.

The effect of leftover hurt and wounds from this kind of emotional trauma is where we need to be careful in our perception of things. Emotional wounds can skew our perceptions when we have not forgiven a person nor allowed the Lord to heal us of painful circumstances. As this woman allowed God to heal her, she became much more discerning in her dating relationships and more able to recognize a similar deceptive pattern. Today she is happily married to a wonderful man—one of God's choosing.

In the body of Christ and among leaders there is a tendency to lean on our own understanding in how we view our circumstances and factor out the spiritual aspect. I do believe it is important to keep a healthy balance in how we view things. But sometimes in our zeal to avoid being overly spiritual we go too far in the other direction and completely ignore the spiritual perspective. It is important not to dismiss prophetic insight too quickly. As a pastor, your negative attitude may discourage an intercessor from ever submitting spiritual discernment to you. Instead, as a prophetic revelation is submitted to you, be encouraged to seek the Lord about it. If you still do not agree, at least you have sought the mind of the Lord about the revelation and also kept the respect of the intercessor.

Just as pastors need to be careful not to dismiss spiritual discernment too quickly, intercessors also need to be sensitive about when to submit a prophetic word. Intercessors, trust God to deal with things in His time and in His way, whether or not your discernment is ever received by leadership. Be open to the possibility that you may be wrong. If yours is a true revelation, God will accomplish what he wants through it. Pastors, just be mindful that intercessors often perceive things before others in the body of Christ. This includes the leadership at times, because of how the Holy Spirit alerts intercessors to pray.

Perception #7: Intercessors are only called to pray

Sometimes church leaders view intercessors as only having a heart to pray and fail to recognize any other spiritual gift beyond prayer and intercession. I personally have resisted being labeled an intercessor for that very reason. Although prayer and intercession is a very strong element in my call, it is not the fullness. In addition to prayer and intercession, I am also called as a pastor and a teacher in the body of Christ and have other spiritual gifts as well. Unfortunately prayer seems to carry with it a connotation that often makes it difficult to see other areas of spiritual gifts or ministry.

Usually intercession is only a part of how a person is called. Sometimes the people who can minister most effectively in evangelistic outreaches, deliverance ministry, altar ministry, counseling, and so on, are the intercessors. They have such a burden to minister and bless others. This is because they carry the heart of the Lord in a special way as they are called to intercede. When they pray, they often experience a strong sense of God's perspective and emotion that releases a tremendous compassion in their heart for others. This is why many intercessors seek other outlets for ministry beyond intercession. They have developed a passion to minister that was born in the prayer closet.

Perception #8: Prophetic Intercessors tend not to attend corporate prayer

Many times a prophetic intercessor avoids a corporate prayer setting because there is no outlet for his or her prophetic expression. As we have discussed, general and prophetic intercessors pray very differently. Can general and prophetic intercessors pray together? Absolutely! These two types of intercessors can pray together most effectively if the prayer time is structured properly within a prayer group or a corporate prayer meeting. It really helps if some ground rules are established that both can agree to.

As we discussed earlier, prophetic intercessors also have a difficult time with people who change prayer points too quickly. Moving from point to point can actually frustrate prophetic intercessors and cause them to avoid attending corporate prayer. They honestly believe they can pray more effectively on their own or with other intercessors who pray as they do. On the other hand, when the prayer focus is strictly prophetic, general intercessors may feel less effective in prayer because they are not getting prophetic revelation and may think they are not a valued part of the prayer time. Both types of intercessors are hearing from the Lord, but their prayer flow is different.

When a prayer meeting is going to include a mix of prophetic and non-prophetic people, a helpful guideline is for everyone to pray prayers that stay on topic and allow the prayer leader determine when to move on to the next prayer point. In this setting, people should not spend a long time praying on any particular prayer point—just a few minutes. Then everyone can pray in agreement together. This arrangement works well in both a small group or in a church-wide prayer meeting.

Perception #9: I must be prophetic in order to discern the revelation given to me by the prophetic intercessors

What do you do, as a pastor, when a prophetic intercessor tells you her or his prophetic sense about yourself or the church? Regardless of whether you are prophetic or not, you still can discern what comes from the Spirit of God and what does not. Let me also say that I believe that God gives pastors an extra measure of discernment, because pastors have a call to watch over the souls of the people in their congregation. Because of the authority and accountability that comes with this call, I believe pastors have a heightened spiritual sense to discern truth from error.

If someone gives you a prophetic word, there are several things to keep in mind.

- Judge if the prophecy lines up with scriptural principles.

- Discern or ask God for discernment about the spirit in which it was given.

- Consider how you feel about this word, whether you are at peace or uneasy.

If everything seems okay and you have peace in your spirit, then what should you do?

- Bring this prophecy before the Lord and ask Him what He wants you to do.

- Ask the Lord about the timing of when something needs to be implemented.

- Ask the Lord to confirm this word to you in other ways.

I always have found that if a prophecy is really from God, He does confirm it in several ways. For example, God can confirm the prophecy circumstantially, through other trusted friends and associates approaching you with the same word, scriptures that start popping out at you as you read, and so on.

Perception #10 I'm uncomfortable when intercessors justify praying for disaster to come if it brings revival.

There are many prophecies today that connect God to judgment supposedly to release a revival. Although I know God can use any disaster to bring about his purposes,[86] I am uncomfortable with justifying the need for a disaster in order to see revival. Intercessors tend to be a little more sensitive to areas of sin in society because of how sin grieves the Father's heart. Because of this sensitivity to sin, sometimes a subtle anger makes intercessors vulnerable to agreeing with prophecies of judgment and impending catastrophes. The deception is in how intercessors are tempted to agree with a disaster happening because of the promise that God will use it to bring revival. This should never be the position of an intercessor!

---

[86] Romans 8:28

"So I sought for a man among them who would make a wall, and stand in the gap before Me on behalf of the land, that I should not destroy it; but I found none." Ezekiel 22:30

Here is a good example of how God searches for someone to pray for mercy because of the sin discovered in the land. It is not God's desire to bring judgment, but He must judge sin because He is holy. Yet, deeper still in the heart of God is a passion to redeem sinners[87]. This is the motivation of God as He searches for a person who will stand in the gap and pray for restoration. For this reason, an intercessor must always take the position of praying for grace and mercy in the face of impending judgment.

Whenever I hear of prophecies of impending judgment, I am reminded of the story of Jonah. Jonah was a prophet who God told to deliver a prophecy of destruction coming soon to Nineveh. Jonah despised the Ninevites because of their past cruelty towards Israel. Yet, when God asked Jonah to deliver this message, he ran away instead. Why would Jonah refuse to give this kind of prophecy when he hated the Ninevites anyway? After all, the prophecy contained no exhortation to repent in order to avert this judgment.

Although the warning carried no call to repent, Jonah knew God's character well enough to know that when he spoke this warning, it could produce the opposite of what Jonah wanted to

---

[87] Reference Chapter 4

see happen. Jonah wanted God to judge Nineveh because he was angry with its people. So God had to deal with Jonah's heart in the same way he has to deal with ours when we are angry at the sinful ways we see in others. God's heart is always to redeem which is why we must allow God to fill us with His grace and mercy in our response to society. The story of Jonah always encourages me to remember that no matter how deeply a city or a nation deserves judgment, God's heart is always to look for someone who is willing to stand in the gap so that He can bring restoration[88].

Perception #11 The tendency to view our spiritual gift or calling as more important than another.

All Christians need to be careful of the danger of elevating themselves, their spiritual gift, or their ministry above someone else. Unfortunately, spiritual pride is a particularly sensitive issue between pastors and intercessors. Because of pride and its many forms, the value placed on prayer has been diminished in some local churches.

"For I say through the grace given to me, to everyone who is among you, not to think of himself more highly than he ought to think, but to think soberly, as God has dealt to each one a measure of faith." Romans 12:3

The point of Paul's exhortation is to remember that we are many members of one body and to keep that in mind as we

---

[88] Reference Chapter 4

serve the Lord in our respective roles with our spiritual gifts. Therefore, we are strongly encouraged to appreciate the differing members so that we can work together in unity.

"For we have many members in one body, but all the members do not have the same function, so we, being many, are one body in Christ, and individually members of one another. Having then gifts differing according to the grace that is given to us, let us use them."   Romans 12:4-6a

Unfortunately, both pastors and intercessors have been guilty at times of thinking of their spiritual gift or position as superior. Part of the problem comes from comparing the importance of one gift to another. God has graced the members of His body each with his or her own unique function and purpose. How can a hand say to a foot, "I have no need of you"? How can we determine which part of the body is more valuable when God has determined all parts are needed for the body's proper function? For this reason, the Bible warns us that such comparisons are not wise.

"For we dare not class ourselves or compare ourselves with those who commend themselves. But they, measuring themselves by themselves, and comparing themselves among themselves, are not wise."   2 Corinthians 10:12

When we esteem ourselves as better than someone else, a deception comes into our perception of ourselves and others that is out of alignment with how God sees our position in the body of Christ. Our resulting attitudes and behaviors cause much discord as well as offense among God's people. The source of this deception really is spiritual pride.

Too little confidence, I might add, is just as prideful and dangerous as overconfidence in the life of a believer. Neither position aligns with the biblical statement of our identity in Christ nor embraces the proper relationship we are to have with other members in the body of Christ. The danger with under-confidence becomes clear when you try to encourage a person with too little confidence—you soon discover that pendulum swings quickly from under-confidence to overconfidence and back again. Words of encouragement for the under-confident person can become like a bottomless pit that is never completely satisfied. The words act like a temporary patch to mask the real issue. That is not to say that we should never encourage someone with a lack of confidence. We should look for opportunities to encourage and build up one another as we are exhorted in I Thessalonians 5:11. We just need to be careful how we go about encouraging others.

The question we should consider is this, "In what way are we encouraging our brothers and sisters?"

Are we building up a person's confidence to rely upon her or his own strength, understanding, and abilities or in God's? Unfortunately, many well-meaning Christians enable what can become a cyclical pattern of under-confidence. What we must recognize is beneath this apparent lack of confidence is an incorrect view of one's spiritual identity. The real issue needing to be addressed is pride and there is only one remedy for pride: repentance.

The danger of this incorrect perception is in the way it influences our view of others. As a result of incorrect perceptions, pastors and intercessors have sometimes been guilty of not valuing one another as a vital part in the body of Christ. Pride is an ugly sin that says, "I do not need anyone; I do not even need God. I can do it on my own."

The opposite of under-confidence is overconfidence in one's perceived ability, sense of self-importance, or intellect that brings about divisions in the body of Christ. It is a self-centered attitude of superiority that does not consider the impact of one's words, actions, or decisions upon others around them. It happens in such deceptive, subtle ways that we sometimes fail to recognize a prideful attitude in ourselves.

A major doorway for pride to enter our lives is through unhealed emotional pain and trauma. When spiritual pride is working in our lives as a result of unhealed offenses, we can even use the faults and shortcomings of others as an excuse to justify our own wrong attitudes. Prideful mindsets, in turn, become strong wedges that divide and keep us separated from others. When someone is insecure, often pride manifests in a need to prove oneself. Unfortunately others may be put down in the process of one's insatiable desire for approval.

Intellectual pride views others as less significant when knowledge itself is highly esteemed. The Bible warns us of this incorrect valuing of knowledge.

"Knowledge puffs up, but love edifies."　　*I Corinthians 8:1b*

In other words, knowledge is beneficial only when it is coupled with love. Love is the necessary balance for knowledge because knowledge without love becomes pride. Since pride can become such a deceptive blind spot in our lives, we must remain open to God revealing any hidden area of pride in our lives, especially during times of promotion or relational conflicts.

Sometimes intercessors have been guilty of pride in their attitude toward pastors or other church leaders. Because of the prophetic insight God reveals to intercessors, sometimes they perceive themselves as having great wisdom and forget God is the true source of this wisdom. Through this deception, attitudes can develop that lead intercessors into thinking they are more spiritually aware than their pastors or other believers. So then, prophetic intercessors get the mistaken idea that they are called to instruct the pastor on how to lead the church. Although it is true that God does use prophetic intercessors to confirm or even bring significant prophetic insight, it is the heart attitude of the intercessor that matters. For this reason, it is particularly important to see our prophetic gift in the right biblical perspective, which is that we are just one part of the body of Christ that makes up the whole. Other members are just as important in bringing about the proper functioning of the whole body.

What has complicated this issue and has wounded intercessors is that prayer and prophetic intercession has not always been understood or valued within the local church. Intercessors sometimes have encountered an attitude among church leaders that prayer is not a necessary part of the work of the ministry, or worse, treated intercessors as the part of the body to be avoided. Because this has caused such deep wounds in intercessors, I am going to take the opportunity to explain this in more detail. My intention is not to judge pastors, but rather to expose how words, actions, and perceptions have sent a wrong message to intercessors. For many church leaders, the harm has been completely unintentional.

For instance, misunderstanding can occur when pastors are invited to attend a prayer meeting. Pastors many times assume that they are obligated to lead the meeting because that is what pastors do—they lead. Even though this is ultimately the pastor's decision and needs to be respected, misunderstandings can happen through the attitude in which the decision is made. It is really helpful to discuss the order of the meeting with the intercessory leader beforehand. When a pastor is present, people naturally defer to his or her leadership. However, my encouragement to pastors is this. If you want to have an opportunity to really understand and connect with intercessors, try just sitting in and being a part of a prayer meeting rather than leading it. You may discover some valuable insights about your intercessors and how they serve in prayer.

For some pastors, sitting through an intercessory prayer meeting may take you beyond your comfort zone, especially if you are not used to spending time with intercessors. I know most pastors are typically very busy people and are very conscious of time. One word of caution I would like to offer, especially to busy pastors who are used to leading most of the meetings they attend. Be particularly careful to resist any temptation to become fidgety, impatient, or bored when you are not leading a prayer meeting. If you are feeling pressured because of time constraints, it would be better to let the intercessors know beforehand that you have only a certain amount of time and then you have to excuse yourself. As with most people, intercessors want to feel that you really want to be there. So a key to building your relationship with intercessors is in fully engaging with them during the time you are there. Most intercessors would not have any problem with you needing to leave early if you have told them. In fact, knowing that you are busy causes them to be even more appreciative of the time you have set in your schedule to be with them. This communicates your value of them in a tangible way.

Intercessors have difficulty when the value of prayer is not embraced by the entire leadership team. Although all of us would agree that prayer is a good thing, some church leaders have treated prayer as an afterthought until a crisis occurs. Then suddenly prayer becomes temporarily important. When the crisis is over, then it is back to business as usual. This attitude communicates a mixed message of the proper valuing of prayer to the body of Christ. The apostle Paul's exhortation is for all believers to pray unceasingly. From this scripture, it is clear that prayer is one of the foundational Christian disciplines we are to maintain[89].

As with ALL of us, sometimes church leaders have been guilty of pride in how they talk about the importance of what they do, how successful they are, and what they have accomplished as leaders. Boasting in the Lord is not a problem. When we boast in ourselves with an attitude of superiority and self-promotion, there is an issue. You would be amazed how many times leaders have boasted in front of intercessors, while at the same time demeaning the importance of prayer. This display truly breaks the heart of an intercessor. Along with pride is usually an underlying attitude that says to the intercessor, "I can do this without you. What you do is really not necessary to the success of this ministry."

This treatment affects intercessors in two ways. Not only do they feel devalued personally, they are also grieved because of the way this attitude impacts the continued effectiveness of the ministry. Because of their call to seek God in prayer,

---

[89] 1 Thessalonians 5:17

intercessors tend to have an acute awareness of how it really is not our human wisdom or ability that accomplishes great things in God. Rather, our success depends on how well we rely on and trust God as our source of strength and wisdom[90].

Needless to say, when prayer is not valued in the culture of the local church, intercessors do not feel valued either. They tend to view other ministries as having a greater place of importance because of the lack of emphasis or place given to prayer within the life of the local church. Unfortunately, church leaders have even made statements about how *real* ministry takes place in the ministries that are directly touching people's lives, such as the youth ministry, children's ministry, and evangelistic outreaches. This is part of the underlying attitude in the church today that has deeply grieved those who recognize the importance of prayer and have been willing to pray anyway. Often when leaders have not seen the connection between prayer and effective ministry, prayer is not valued as a vital ministry. As a result of this perception, time, energy, and even finances are not seen as important investments in developing the prayer ministry within the local church.

Prayer is a necessary backbone to a local church advancing in effective ministry and is most definitely one of the vehicles God uses to impact people's lives. Jesus himself is our greatest example of this.

---

[90] Psalm 144:1

"He always lives to make intercession on behalf of them."

Hebrews 7:25b

For whom does Jesus intercede? He intercedes for all who come to God through Him. Not only is Jesus interceding for the advancement of His church, but he is actually modeling for us an essential key in furthering His kingdom—prayer. It is certainly not my intention to elevate prayer as more important than any other ministry. Instead I would like to suggest that our perception of prayer needs to change. The ministry of prayer needs to come into its rightful place within the local church as one of the foundational elements necessary to reach the lost and dying people of this world.

In sharing these perceptions of how words and actions can be negatively perceived it has been my hope to create a place of understanding for both pastors and prophetic intercessors. In order for this understanding to truly be beneficial it must also be coupled with the right biblical view of the body of Christ. Let us also recognize pride as a dangerous enemy that opposes a correct biblical perception.

As we relate to the body of Christ, it is important that we embrace the understanding of how our real identity is in Christ and not in our spiritual gift, in our calling, or in the position we hold. Although it is true that some parts are hidden while other are more visible, this does not make one part better than the other or more valuable. Paul has an interesting perspective about this in Corinthians.

*"But now God has set the members, each one of them, in the body just as He pleased. And if they were all one member, where would the body be? But now indeed there are many members, yet one body. And the eye cannot say to the hand, 'I have no need of you'; nor again the head to the feet, 'I have no need of you.' No, much rather, **those members which seem weaker are necessary.** And **those members of the body which we think to be less honorable, on these we bestow greater honor,** and our un-presentable parts have greater modesty, but our presentable parts have no need. But **God composed the whole body, having given greater honor to that part that lacks it, that there should be no schism in the body,** but that the members should have the same care for one another. And if one member suffers, all members suffer with it; or if one member is honored, all the members rejoice with it."*

1 Corinthians 12:18-26

In Conclusion

It is my intention and prayer that in reading the pages of this chapter we have cracked open a window of understanding so that we might to take a fresh look into the heart of an intercessor, the many challenges pastors and intercessors each face, how prayer is connected to effective ministry, and the importance of the way we are called to function together as the body of Christ. We have seen how pride seeks to divide that which God has created to be interdependent—the body of Christ! More specifically, pride seeks to divide the connection between pastors and intercessors. The enemy knows that when the church is functioning together with all its members, the body increases in strength and power to overcome all the strategies of the wicked one. Unity is what Satan most fears and is why his opposition is so fierce.

"And I say to you that you are Peter, and on this rock I will build my church and the gates of hell shall not prevail against it."

Matthew 16:18

Launching a Prophetic Intercession Team

"Unless the Lord builds the house, they labor in vain who build it."   Psalm 127:1a

The real key to building anything with lasting value is in allowing God to be the master builder and learning how to partner with him in the process. As with anything new, what you pour into the initial foundation of a team is crucial to the quality and strength of what is produced. We will explore some things to consider in laying the initial foundation of a prophetic intercessory team. We will discuss various aspects of what the team structure should look like as well as team values that I have found essential in building and maintaining a healthy team. Of course, many of these principles can be applied to other types of prayer teams or small groups. However, my primary focus is prophetic intercession and it is the emphasis of the following discussion.

An Essential First Step

Before we begin, let me emphasize that an essential first step is to acquire the blessing and support of your church leadership before you establish a team. I have found that there is a great blessing and a spiritual enabling to effectively lead a team when things are done in the right order.

Team Structure

In considering the team structure five areas need defining: Vision, Mission Statement, Commitment and Expectations, Team Member Approval Process, and Team Values.

I. Vision

Creating a vision statement is essential for a team to understand why it exists and what it does. A vision statement should be broad enough to cover the basic prayer assignment but not include the specific details for accomplishing the vision. It is important to articulate this vision statement so that anyone on the team can simply answer one question. "What is the vision for your team?"

For example, one answer could be this statement. "Our prayer team is called to watch and pray over the apostolic vision of our church."

In principle, a vision statement is very similar to a topic sentence for an essay. Everything following the topic sentence is written to support and answer the reasons why the topic sentence is true. The same is true with a vision statement. All of the team activities should reflect back to the original vision statement. This affords a sense of ongoing purpose and direction for the team.

A vision statement should be presented to everyone at the start of a new prayer team. The vision defines the reason for coming and the framework of the assignment. When a vision statement is unclear or the nature of the meetings does not line up with the statement, leaders will find that people become confused and question why they are there. Usually people join a team because they agree with the team's vision. The vision becomes the basis of their commitment. If that vision changes without a proper transition process, they may begin to feel, "Wait a minute, this is not what I agreed to!" It is important to clearly articulate a vision that is broad enough to allow for growth, yet still establishes a general framework.

II. Mission Statement

A mission statement is meant to further clarify and define the purpose for the team and what it hopes to accomplish. For example, "The mission of our team is to serve as watchmen over how the Lord desires to fulfill the church vision in advancing His kingdom."

You may want to further explain by saying, "We are focusing on three things: watching how the Holy Spirit is moving, discerning any spiritual opposition, and then praying agreement with the Lord's strategy in moving forward."

The important thing is that a mission statement should clarify how this vision will be carried out.

III. Commitment and Team Expectations

In the formation of any team, people need to understand what is being asked of them. It is important to explain what is involved in joining a team so each person can evaluate whether or not they can fulfill the team requirements. Some of the questions to be determined are time, location, and team expectations. Included with these concerns are other important personal aspects, such as imparting godly values that help to create a safe environment.

Creating a Safe Environment

Creating the right kind of atmosphere has to do, in part, with the location of the meetings. The best location is a central one that everyone can easily access, although is not always possible. Many prayer groups choose to meet in a church building. My preference is to meet in someone's home rather than in a church building. A home provides hospitality and helps create a warm, safe atmosphere that sets people at ease. When I first began our prophetic intercession team, we met in my home. I would pull out my China tea service and prepare a light snack. Our times together in those early days were characterized by a lot of laughter, sharing of hearts, ministering to one another, establishing guidelines, foundational training, and prayer.

In the beginning, I would recommend meeting weekly. One reason is to begin team building. Many times intercessors are a little timid about praying prophetically with others they do not know very well, so it is important to spend time getting to know one another. Creating a safe environment is vital to help the ministry team relax with each other and freely express the prophetic gifts that God has placed in each one. So I encourage a family atmosphere where people understand that group prayer is a learning environment. It is okay to make mistakes, be yourself, and expect to be loved unconditionally.

Part of creating a safe place also means establishing clear boundaries. I recommend using the first few months to train the team in prophetic intercession and establish clear guidelines for the prayer meetings[91]. During this phase, I would suggest keeping the prayer points general when praying for the church. In other words, avoid entering into any significant spiritual warfare other than to pray general prayers of protection. Of course, much depends on the maturity level of the intercessors and how the Lord is leading you to develop the team.

The Team Preparation Process

The training process for our prophetic intercession team was about eight weeks. I had a strong sense from the Lord that we needed to begin by laying a foundation with teaching, training, and team building. Although now we have a wonderful prayer team of men and women, we began with a team of ten ladies. Many of these women were coming from very hurtful backgrounds and we needed time to build relationships, trust

---

[91] Reference Chapter 3

levels, and pray for healing as we prepared ourselves for this ministry.

Could we have just come together and prayed rather than going through this preparation process? Yes, but I think we would have missed the way the Lord wanted to build this team. There were things that I believe God wanted to work in us personally and as a team. It is like the stages you go through before marriage. First, there is courtship, engagement, and then marriage. If a couple submits to God's timing and preparation process, they learn that in each phase are secret joys and truths that God wants to reveal to them. God wants an opportunity to teach us how to best relate to another person and give us His understanding as to what it really means to love. These truths, woven together in the process of time, are intended to become part of the fabric of a healthy marriage.

In principle, it is never a good idea to short circuit God's preparation process. We may get to our intended goal quicker, but we will have missed how God wanted to best prepare us. The same is true in building a team, the team leader needs to seek the Lord's wisdom about this initial stage.

One final thought—although our team began with women, it is important to include our intercessory brothers as well. The men that the Lord has raised up over the years to be part of our team have added a necessary and unique dimension to prophetic intercession. Be sure not to overlook these precious brothers when you consider putting together a team. They add a balance and perspective that gives a greater wisdom in how we pray. Somehow we have gotten the wrong idea in the body of Christ that prayer and intercession is mostly a woman's role. Not so! Our best example of an intercessor is Jesus himself[92].

Intercessors Need Pastoral Care

Another aspect of creating a safe environment is to provide an avenue for the intercessors to receive pastoral care and ministry. An often overlooked fact is that prayer warriors bare the brunt of spiritual attack for the people and situations for whom they are interceding. Sometimes intercessors may not understand or know how to respond to spiritual retaliation and need instruction. In a very real sense, they are battling on the front lines and encounter strong spiritual opposition. During seasons of intense warfare, it is easy for them to get off-track, lose perspective, and feel overwhelmed by what they discern or experience.

So when intercessors are feeling battle weary or experience personal challenges of their own, who ministers to them? This is an important question when you consider the spiritual health of prayer warriors. As a Prayer Pastor, I find that I have many roles in ministering to these needs. There are times that I need to spend training and equipping intercessors so that their foundation in the Word is firm as they learn to war effectively. Sometimes they need counsel and comfort if they feel overwhelmed when they experience new levels of the prophetic

---

[92] Hebrews 7:25

or spiritual warfare. Often I give counsel to help intercessors discern visions, dreams, or spiritual opposition they encounter. Other times I find myself praying for personal issues that need prayer or guidance.

Unfortunately, many prayer leaders communicate a message to intercessors that personal prayer needs are to be left at the door, so that the group can focus on the *real* prayer assignment. Although you do not want a prayer meeting to be sidelined with personal needs, it is important to establish a way for intercessors to be cared for as well. There are several ways that this can be done.

Allow For Times of Personal Ministry

One question I keep in mind as each of the team members arrive is, "How are they doing?" I specifically watch for a spirit of heaviness about them or if their countenance appears downcast. They may be experiencing some spiritual warfare or are troubled in their spirit about some personal issues. Then, I ask the Lord if I need to pray for them before the meeting begins or can it wait until after.

I have learned that if people are heavily burdened, weighed down by their circumstances, or experiencing strong spiritual opposition, it often hinders them from being able to enter into prayer during the meeting. There have been times when the Lord has told me to lay aside the meeting agenda and minister prophetically to the team. This is a great way to encourage and build up the team.

When I am sensing that the Lord wants to minister prophetically to the team, there are a few ways that I do this. Sometimes my team assistant and I pray over each person. Sometimes I ask other team members to prophesy during this time of personal ministry. When I include the team in ministering, I allow fifteen minutes of personal ministry. Believe me, it becomes quite a challenge to limit the time when the team is activated prophetically. Other times I pray a prophetic sense over the team as a whole rather than individually.

Every so often, when I sense the Lord releasing us into a new level of prophetic prayer, I take the opportunity to call forth any prophetic gifts the Lord is stirring within the team. When the team prays for me, I always put my assistant in charge to watch over the prophecies as they come forth. This just helps to maintain the order. Of course, we usually record or take notes of any prophetic words. Because these ministry times usually are prompted spontaneously by the Holy Spirit, prophetic words are recorded by handwritten notes.

These times of prophetic ministry are so valuable to building up and encouraging the team. As mentioned before, intercessors encounter a lot of spiritual opposition as a result of interceding for others, especially when praying protection for the church. Ministering prophetically is a great tool in releasing spiritual refreshment to them. The other benefit is it is an opportunity to listen to what the Lord is speaking over each person. It helps us to know each other according to the Spirit and how to keep one another in prayer.

Another effective way to minister to the team is to divide people into small groups or assign partners. This is an effective way to develop more of a team mentality in meeting personal needs of one another.

When people need further ministry or counsel, they are free to approach me after the meeting, especially if the request is private. My strong exhortation to any prayer leader is to be watchful in caring for the personal needs of your intercessors. It is important intercessors do not get the message that we just expect them to perform their prayer assignment and not care for them personally.

Finally, create times when the team can have fun together. Spiritual refreshing is good, but also it is important to minister to the soul. Having fun nights is a good way to get together, especially during the summer or holidays. We have had a variety of events such as bowling, swim parties, movie nights, board games, and pot lucks just to spend time together having fun. It is important to connect on personal levels by planning activities outside of the normal prayer gatherings.

Attendance

When intercessors want to join the team, I strongly encourage them to make regular attendance a priority. Unlike a home fellowship, a prophetic intercession team is a ministry calling not just a time of fellowship. If you are called as a prophetic intercessor with an assignment to watch and pray over the vision of the church, do not consider it a casual assignment to attend sporadically. It is a watchman role with a prayer watch to maintain. Of course, there is grace for times when "real life" happens and there is a legitimate reason for not attending or even when a well deserved sabbatical is needed.

My perspective is that missing a meeting should be an exception, not a regular pattern. I really believe that the role of a watchman carries with it a responsibility to maintain the prayer watch that God has assigned. If you know that you are called to be on this kind of a team, it is important to be faithful to that call. Other team members are affected when someone does not show up and does not say why.

From time to time, I have had to confront this issue and have found that often people get overcommitted in other areas of ministry. So in trying to reestablish balance, they rob Peter to pay Paul as the expression goes. So, I encourage such people to seek the Lord about their ministry commitment and to be clear how the Lord wants them to invest their time and energy. If their ministry season is changing and they need to be released from the team, that is fine as long as they know what God is requiring.

Other Team Expectations

Other team expectations involve things such as fasting, prayer assignments, finding personal intercessors, and receiving e-mail updates.

Coming with Hearts Prepared

Coming to a prayer meeting with your heart prepared to enter into a time of intercession can greatly impact the effectiveness of the prayer time (see prophetic prayer guidelines in chapter 3). This is true in any ministry. Here are a few things that I have asked intercessors to make a regular practice. Most of them should be done daily.

- Praying in tongues

- Fasting one day per week

- Spending time in praise and worship

- Maintaining a daily devotional time to pray and seek God

- Spending time in the Word of God

- Casting your daily cares onto the Lord:

- Forgive anyone who has offended you

- Getting enough rest

All of these are important aspects of maintaining a healthy spiritual life that will both refresh and sensitize your spirit to the Holy Spirit. Praying in tongues, regular fasting, and praise and worship are amazing tools in developing and maintaining a spiritual sharpness prophetically. Each helps to sensitize your spirit to the Spirit of God. Forgiveness and learning to cast your cares daily is a way to protect us from carrying more burdens than God intends and being weighed down mentally. As we release our cares and concerns to the Lord, not only does God have opportunity to work in our circumstances, but also our spirit is better able to hear the Lord and respond more freely in the way the Holy Spirit is moving. Maintaining a daily devotional time and spending time in the Word of God is like positioning the rudder of a sailboat—it helps to set the course for the day. Reading and meditating in the Word causes our thoughts to align with the mind of Christ. Daily intimate time with the Lord is so vital in preparing our minds to face our daily pressures and challenges. Finally, getting adequate rest is essential to maintaining a proper balance in our physical body. Our mental processes and emotional state is greatly impacted when we ignore our physical need for rest. Even our perspective of life is altered when we experience physical weariness or exhaustion.

God has designed man in three parts: spirit, soul, and body. Rest and refreshment are necessary for all three areas. The spirit is strengthened when we are careful to maintain our intimacy with the Lord and are in proper fellowship with others. Our body needs physical rest, proper food, and exercise to function at its best. Our soul, often overlooked, also needs refreshment. How do you refresh the soul? Very simply, leave room in your life for fun! It is very important to take vacations, develop hobbies, or do an activity that is out of the normal pacing of your life.

I encourage our team to pay attention to all eight areas in their daily lives. Of course, we still are human and sometimes no matter how much we try to do the right thing or have the right response, we still have difficult days, experience warfare, and need prayer. So I keep watch over how the team is doing and try to be sensitive about how I can best minister to them as various needs arise.

Team Jobs

Assigning team jobs is a great way to create a sense of ownership for the success of the meeting. Here are the types of responsibilities I assign. We usually have a worship leader who leads us in fifteen to twenty minutes of worship. If you have a worship leader who can flow between worship and intercession, worship can be more of an integral part of the prophetic prayer expression. If you do not have anyone to lead worship, then worship tapes are very helpful. You can designate someone to oversee this area and have her or him put together a series of worship CDs. Each CD should contain a few songs, along with words typed out for people to follow.

On our team we have a scribe to take notes of any prophetic words or revelations that are spoken during the meeting. After the prayer time, these notes are very helpful in capturing the highlights of the prophetic flow and writing a report to our senior pastor. Although there is one main person who does this, we do try to rotate the note-taking responsibility. We also have someone on the team in charge of transcribing any prophetic words that come forth on Sunday morning during our regular church services. Because our services are taped, the transcriber just needs to get a copy and type out any prophecies for that day. These prophetic words are dated and placed in a three-ring binder for reference. I have found this to be a helpful way to continue to pray agreement over significant prophecies spoken over our church.

A team administrator is critical to the administrative functioning of the team. The person who fills this role should be a good communicator, organized, and comfortable with responding quickly by phone or e-mail. Some of the administrator's responsibilities include taking attendance, coordinating birthday cards, sending meeting reminders, forwarding prayer updates to the team, taking meeting notes, and coordinating the food for special events, such as a Christmas party, fun nights, and so on.

Servant Based Training

Early in the development of our team, we implemented something called *servant-based training*. All the team members were expected to rotate in helping to set up and clean up for our meetings and serving in other special projects as these opportunities came. One reason for this plan was to develop the heart of a servant among the team members as they were being mentored prophetically.

Building a Hedge

Intercessors often overlook the need to have people covering them in prayer. So I ask each team member to recruit two or three personal intercessors who are not on the team. These people do not have to be intercessors. They can be anyone who loves them, and are willing to pray regularly.

Within our team we have also have prayer buddies. Everyone is assigned one or two people on the team who they contact weekly to see how things are going, offer encouragement, and cover in prayer. As the team leader, I also keep the team in prayer and ask my team assistants to do the same. During our corporate prayer time, our senior pastor regularly leads the prayer warriors in general prayers of protection over all the ministries. My personal conviction is that it is best to build a hedge of protection in several layers. If each intercessor only has one person praying, then the enemy just has to target that one person and harass her or him so she or he is too distracted to pray. Several layers of prayer cover are best. With several layers of protection, the enemy has greater difficulty in penetrating the hedge.

IV. Team Member Approval Process

The next step in establishing a prophetic intercession team is determining the criteria for team membership. If the team is going to function strictly in prophetic intercession, then anyone who joins should have at least one of the four prophetic gifts. This criterion is not intended to be exclusive. However, I have found that someone who tries to function on a prophetic prayer team without prophetic gifts tends to feel frustrated and left out because she or he has nothing to contribute in the flow of revelation.

Also, when I consider team members, I do not look for people with the most experience or strongest anointing. I look for people who are called to this ministry and who have character traits of being teachable, humble, submissive, and can function as a team player. Some people have been called to our team who were not even aware of how they flow prophetically. It is important for the team leader to discern carefully who is called to the team and how to draw those prophetic gifts out.

Another thing I consider for a prospective team member is church attendance. Does the person regularly attend services, give tithes, and have her or his relationships in order according to Matthew 18.

The process for determining team membership begins with an interview. During the interview, I ask questions about the person's prayer burden. If they are not sure about a prayer burden, I ask them, "What kind of things do you find yourself praying for?" This helps me to discover the person's prayer burden and determine what other prayer teams might be a possibility. Another question I ask, "What kinds of things happen when you pray?" In other words, do they experience visions, impressions, Rhema Words, words of knowledge, words of wisdom, or any kind of prophetic sensing?

One useful tool is a questionnaire designed to reveal any prophetic gifts an intercessor may have (see Appendix A). One sign of a person who is called to be a watchman for the local church is an ongoing burden to pray for the church. As we have discussed previously, watchmen also have an ongoing prophetic sense of the spiritual climate as it relates to the local church or a geographical region. Not every prophetic intercessor has this level of discernment, but a lot of them do.

Sometimes I have a candidate visit our team so I can observe her or his prayer patterns. I also watch the team dynamics to see if this person is a good fit. Several years ago, a couple wanted to join our team whose prophetic gifts did not flow naturally with our team. When I questioned this couple further, I found that their prayer burden was different from the prayer assignment for our team. So, I directed them to another prayer team that turned out to be a better fit for their particular prayer burden.

Part of the process of selecting team members also includes the team leader seeking the Lord about whether someone is called to the team. If I do not know a person very well, I consult with my senior pastor to get his sense about the person. The prophetic intercession team is the only team that I follow stricter criteria in deciding who joins. Due to the prophetic nature of the prayer assignment for this team, I look for those who are able to flow in prophetic intercession and carry a burden to watch and pray over the church vision.

V. Imparting Team Values

The final area has to do with establishing clear guidelines so that people know what to expect and can feel secure. Guidelines are not intended to be inflexible rules, but are put in place to help bring the proper order to our meeting times. Most of these guidelines have been covered in chapter 3. Along with these guidelines are some team values that I encourage in our intercessors.

Value #1 Being Patient with Those Who Are Learning

Occasionally, someone speaks a prophetic word that is off-target. Prophecy can be a mixture of the Holy Spirit, the flesh, and a demonic influence. One time, someone on our team did give a word a word that had a demonic element to it. Everyone on the team sensed it and was wondering how I was going to respond. Fortunately, there was a small part of the word I agreed with, so I guided the team to pray agreement with that part of the word and let the rest go. Later that evening, I pulled the person aside and gently confronted her. She admitted that the word did not feel right to her either. In this case, the person was not trying to be controlling or acting out of order. It was an innocent mistake. She was just young in understanding her prophetic gift. What began in the spirit ended up in the flesh.

There can be a mix of the flesh and the Spirit of God within a prophetic word because of the maturity level of the person. Because of some hurts in this person's life, she began to pray her prophetic sense in the flesh with a demonic spirit resting on her words. Initially, the Holy Spirit did give her a word and if she had just given that portion and stopped it would have been fine. Instead, she continued in her own understanding and that made her vulnerable to the demonic.

I learned an important lesson from this experience. Although I addressed the problem of the mixture right away, I did not let the team members know that I had given correction. It caused the team to feel insecure until I realized I needed to reassure them that the situation had been resolved. It also became a teachable moment to reaffirm that our team is a safe place for learning where people can make mistakes and not be afraid about how they will be corrected. It also underscores the point that we need to be patient with one another and learn to extend grace because we all still are learning.

Value #2 Learning to Value One Another

Although we have discussed this previously, let me repeat the importance of preferring and deferring to one another[93]. It means we do not talk over each other, we allow someone else to go first, and we wait until someone is finished praying before we jump in. We are all part of the body of Christ and we all are

---

[93] Romans 12:10

needed to strengthen the body as a whole. Especially on a prophetic intercession team when we are praying about a certain situation, the Lord uses several of the team members to bring increasing prophetic clarity during the prayer flow. I call this prophetic prayer building. As we begin to pray for a particular prayer point, each of us may get a part of the revelation. Putting the parts together creates a picture of what God is revealing to us. This is God's wisdom for us to understand what He is saying about a situation and also how to pray more effectively. From this, God often shows us prayer strategies about how to war effectively. What I am describing is like putting a puzzle together. Each piece has an important place in helping to make sense the picture that is forming. Each of us has a part of prophetic insight that contributes to the overall effectiveness of the prayer session.

Value #3 Valuing the Differing Prophetic Streams

Even within the realm of the prophetic there are differences in prophetic expression. Probably the greatest difference is between those who have a strong gift of the discernment of spirits and those who have the gift of prophecy. As we have discussed, the discernment of spirits involves a feeling aspect with many of the five senses activated. So when people are discerning a demonic spirit, they are actually feeling its presence in the spiritual atmosphere. Someone who has the gift of prophecy does not usually experience this feeling aspect. One functioning in the gift of Prophecy hears a word from the

Lord and then declares what they have heard. One kind of prophetic expression is not better than the other. All kinds are necessary in the full expression of the body of Christ. We need to be careful to learn to value and appreciate the differences that each body part represents and not gravitate only to the part of the body that we feel the most comfortable with or can best relate to.

Value #4 Team Connections

Another important value is for the team to develop connections with other team members. Sometimes people join a prayer team just because they like the leader and want to connect with the person more closely. What I try to discourage is *only* connecting with the leader. A team becomes strong when people let themselves love and connect with each other. The team experience becomes much richer as they discover and value the other members. This kind of inner-connectedness also allows me to develop leadership within the team so that I can step away and it does not impact the cohesiveness of the team. I try to avoid letting members develop an unhealthy dependency on me as a leader. When you consider the idea of establishing multiple teams, this issue becomes very important.

In Conclusion

A prophetic intercession team can greatly benefit the local church, but taking the time to establish a healthy foundation is essential to its effectiveness. In this chapter I have shared insights about the process I experienced in developing a prophetic intercessory team. I offer them only as suggestions. The real key is to ask the Lord to guide you. For each church, the Lord may cause a prophetic intercession team to develop a little differently from how someone else has done it. Leave room for God to tailor this prophetic expression to the needs of your local church.

Ellen Laitinen

The Importance of a Pastoral Prayer Shield

"The eyes of the Lord search the whole Earth in order to strengthen those whose hearts are fully committed to Him."

2 Chronicles 16:9a (NLT)

Today, society is laced with strong temptations that war against our minds, moral character, and biblical standards of holiness. Unfortunately, many congregations have experienced the devastation of a leader who has given in to sexual immorality, financial misappropriations, and/or selfish ambition. James 3:16 reveals, "*wherever there is jealousy and selfish ambition, there you will find disorder and evil of every kind.*" The impact to a congregation in a leader yielding to these carnal temptations is an open door to anger, disillusionment, fear, and offense. The emotional damage and chaos this creates is why the sheep scatter, many of whom never recover from this level of betrayal and heartache. Although pastors and leaders have a moral responsibility to walk in integrity before God, the body of Christ also has a duty to pray for all those in authority over them. In this chapter, I will cover several aspects in how to effectively pray, protect, and administrate prayer coverage for your senior pastor and pastoral team.

A Call to Prayer

"I urge you, first of all to pray for all people. Ask God to help them; intercede for them on their behalf, and give thanks for them. Pray this way for kings and all those in authority so that we can live peaceful and quiet lives marked by godliness and dignity." 1 Timothy 2:1-2 (NLT)

In this passage, the Lord is specific in how we are to pray for leaders. We are exhorted to pray for God to help them, intercede on their behalf, and give thanks for them because this is God's established authority. When we honor and pray for our leaders we are actually honoring God and his order of things. As a result, a promise of "peaceful, quiet lives marked by godliness" is activated in our lives.

Although it may appear that many of our pastors are strong in the Lord and do not appear to have any visible problems, it is a mistake to assume that our leaders do not need us to pray for them or for leaders to think that they have no need for prayer. All of us deal with the challenges, pressure, and spiritual opposition that come with daily living. There is a reason God is exhorting his people to pray in this way. It is because in His design of the body of Christ, prayer is necessary in maintaining its proper health and functioning. There is also an interesting promise connected with this exhortation to pray for our leaders and, as with most promises, it is conditional. The promise has to do with living peaceful and quiet lives. It comes as a result of "if we will pray" for our leaders and those in authority over us. God has purposely designed the body of Christ to be inter-dependant with each joint supplying a need that brings strength to the whole body. It is important that we do not view our pastors as a separate entity that does not need the strength from rest of the body. Nothing could be further than the truth. The fact is, for pastoral leadership to fully be empowered to accomplish the purposes of God in their lives, they need to be rightly connected to the body of Christ. It takes all of us functioning together in the body for us to mature into the fullness of God in Christ.

"He makes the whole body fit together perfectly. As each part does its own special work, it helps the other parts to grow, so that the whole body is healthy and growing, and full of love."

Ephesians 4:16 (NIV)

The Importance of Prayer Coverage

Prayer is foundational to the church advancing in kingdom purposes. We know from the scriptures that before the foundation of the world that God planned good works for us to accomplish in our lives[94]. It's evident that God has a planned purpose for each of our lives. Psalm 37:23 declares, "*The steps of a good man are ordered by the Lord and He delights in his*

---

[94] Ephesians 2:10

way." The word ordered is from the Hebrew word *Kun* and means to establish, prepare, or to make firm. From this definition, there is a sense of confidence that God will direct the path in which we are to walk because of a divine purposing that is being worked out in our lives. Foundational to how we come to understand God's plan for us begins in our communication with Him. This is the reason prayer so important. It is because prayer is a place of hearing and communicating with God as well as discerning His will. We know that our own personal prayer time is important, but what we may not realize is how God also utilizes the prayers of others in helping us to fulfill our destiny. Let's revisit the biblical example of Peter's release from prison.

"Peter was therefore kept in prison, but constant prayer was offered to God for him by the church."   Acts 12:5

Peter had been going about doing the work of the ministry when King Herod decided to arrest him. Herod had already been utilized by the enemy to execute his evil schemes to oppose and harass believers. He also was responsible for killing James, the brother of John. Concerned for Peter's life, the church began to pray fervently and unceasingly for Peter's release. In response to their prayers, the Lord sent an angel to Peter's prison cell.

"Now behold, an angel of the Lord stood by him, and light shone in the prison; and he struck Peter on the side and raised him up saying, 'Arise quickly!' And his chains fell off his hands.

Then the angel said to him, 'Gird yourself and tie on your sandals'; and so he did. And he said to him, 'Put on your garment and follow me.' So he went out and followed him, and did not know that what was done by the angel was real, but thought he was seeing a vision. When they went past the first and the second guard posts, they came to an iron gate that leads to the city, which opened to them of its own accord; and they went out and went down one street, and immediately the angel departed from him."   Acts 12:7-10

This passage paints a very clear picture of the church experiencing very strong warfare as Peter and other church members are continuing to spread the gospel. It is important to understand that this same battle exists for the church today. We have a very real enemy opposing us. For Peter to continue to advance in his ministry, he needed others to intercede for him in pressing forward. Peter's miraculous release was a direct result of the faithful prayers of the saints interceding on his behalf. The intensity of their prayer created an atmosphere of God's presence so powerful, and so much in alignment with the heart of God, that even the answer came in the form of a supernatural experience. Several times throughout the New Testament the Apostle Paul exhorts believers about the importance of prayer in the advancement of the gospel.

"And for me, that utterance may be given to me, that I may open my mouth boldly to make known the mystery of the gospel."   Ephesians 6:19

As an apostolic leader, Paul even requests prayer for himself. He understood the necessity of drawing upon the power of God through the body of Christ by activating prayer and intercession. He specifically asked believers to pray for the Holy Spirit to grant him a greater boldness in sharing the gospel. As we pray for our leaders, not only is there an enabling to defeat the spiritual opposition, but also a greater empowering of the Holy Spirit to minister. This principle of needing prayer coverage is true for all of us, not just for leaders, but this certainly clarifies the necessity of keeping our leadership properly covered in prayer.

Pastoral Prayer Shield

In our church we have several intercessory teams, each with a different prayer focus. Initially, the Prophetic Intercession Team was the team that I utilized to provide on-going prayer coverage for the pastoral staff and ministry directors. In addition to praying over the church vision, each prophetic intercessor has three to four pastors they keep in daily prayer. The intercessors are also expected to fast one day a week and include their assigned pastors, along with other general prayer points, as part of their fasting emphasis for that day. Since each pastor or ministry director oversees several ministries, this is an easy and effective way to keep all the ministries in the church covered in prayer. An important key to this coverage is for each intercessor to fast a different day so that all the days of the week are covered in prayer on a continuous basis.

Expanding the Prayer Shield

Recently, we have expanded our pastoral prayer shield to include all intercessors in the church who have a burden to pray for the leadership. So instead of limiting this assignment to only the Prophetic Intercession Team, we have added another layer of prayer coverage by including all prayer warriors within our congregation. At least once a year, I will utilize our corporate prayer time to present the vision of the pastoral prayer shield and give people an opportunity to sign up. The following is the informational letter I pass out when I am recruiting for this pastoral prayer shield.

Dear Prayer Warriors,

If you have a burden to keep our pastoral staff in prayer on a regular basis, I would like to invite you to become part of our Pastoral Prayer Shield.

Requirements

To sign up you must be a member of the Church, a regular thither, follow Mathew 18 in keeping in right standing in your personal relationships and maintain confidentiality when prayer requests are given to you.

Commitment Level

This commitment is for one year and you will be given an option to renew this commitment each year. You must be willing to keep the pastors you sign-up for in prayer on a regular basis. There will be an e-mail update with specific prayer requests for each pastor once a month. Occasionally, I may send an e-mail request mobilizing prayer for general needs concerning our pastoral staff and church body or activate our calling tree for those rare times when there is an emergency.

Corporate Prayer & Fasting

There are no meetings involved. I would, however, request that you make a priority of attending one of the corporate prayer times: Saturday morning or Pre-Service prayer on Sunday. I would also like to request that you set aside a fasting day, one day a week on an on-going basis to pray for your assigned pastors. Please feel free to fast in whatever way the Lord shows you. This can be all or part of a day with a food fast or some other non-food type of fast. The main idea is to set aside time in prayer. Fasting is a wonderful way of keeping your spirit sensitive to the voice of the Lord and increase your ability to pray effectively!

Please fill out the following information and return the bottom portion of this form to me personally or place in my box.

Together we can see God's kingdom purposes move forward in a mighty way!

Thank you in advance for your willingness to pray!

Many blessings,

Pastor Ellen

....

PASTORAL PRAYER SHIELD

This year I would like to pray for the following pastors. Please choose up to three:

____Pastor D	____Pastor C	____Pastor KE
____Pastor K	____Pastor B	____Pastor A
____Pastor G	____Pastor J	____Pastor M
____Pastor E	____Pastor B	____Pastor N

(Please **PRINT**)

Name:

_____Phone:_____

E-mail:_____

Please **circle** the day you would like to fast weekly:

Monday Tuesday Wednesday Thursday Friday Saturday Sunday

I confirm that I meet the requirements and agree to the 1 year commitment to pray for as outlined.

Signature:

As people sign up, they are placed on an e-mail distribution list so that they can be easily updated with specific prayer needs. This means each pastoral staff member, including our senior pastor and apostle have a team of 15-20 prayer warriors fasting and praying on a regular basis.

I have designated one of my administratively gifted intercessors to coordinate the pastoral prayer requests. She does this by sending an e-mail to our pastoral staff, every three weeks or so, to ask them if they have any current prayer requests. From my experience, I have found that it is easy for pastors to get so busy that they do not remember to update their intercessors on their current prayer needs. I have to say that I have been guilty of this myself! So we have tried to assist in this process by initiating an e-mail to serve as a reminder.

Criteria for Prayer Requests

The criteria for pastoral prayer requests are designed to cover three specific areas of prayer: personal needs, ministry concerns, and immediate family. Personal prayer requests should include health and strength, finances, areas of spiritual attack as well as other personal needs impacting their livelihood. Ministry concerns involve all aspects of ministry growth and effectiveness (that is, more laborers, God's favor in a particular area, time, wisdom and revelation, creativity, strategy, divine appointments and connections). Family prayer requests should include only immediate family members (spouse, children, and parents). Those who are single may include parents and siblings. Alongside of these three areas is also a Pastoral Prayer Guide that I give all the intercessors on the prayer shield. In case we do not have any current prayer requests from some of our pastors, I have a list of general areas that can be prayed for daily. The following are just a sample of the kinds of things we keep in mind as we pray. You may want to add or adapt this according to the needs you discern over your own pastoral team.

Pastoral Prayer Guide

Let us agree daily for:

- The Lord to order their time

- Divine favor

- Divine appointments, opportunities, and connections

- Divine health and strength

- Protection over their families

- Traveling mercies

- The Lord to increase their ministry and send workers

- Abundant financial provision

- Revelation knowledge, wisdom and strategies

- Every scheme of the enemy to be dismantled and broken

- Protection over every form of communication (phones, internet, faxes, sound, electronics, and media equipment)

- An open heaven as they minister or seek the Lord

Processing the Prayer Requests

The pastoral updates are e-mailed to the pastors once a month asking for any current prayer requests they may have. Below is an example of what is generally communicated:

Dear Pastors,

Just checking in to see if you have any prayer requests so that I can update your intercessors.

We count it a joy to serve you in this way!

Many blessings,

Prayer Coordinator

Since I am the associate pastor overseeing the prayer ministry and also pray for the other pastoral staff, I have asked the prayer shield coordinator to include my e-mail address in the copy "cc" section so I can stay updated as well on the incoming prayer requests from the other staff pastors. The pastors can expect to receive an acknowledging e-mail from the prayer coordinator that we have received their request and that their intercessors will be updated.

Confidentiality

Sometimes we receive very confidential prayer requests from our pastoral staff. It is our heart to protect the wording of these requests before they are sent out to the distribution list of intercessors. This is where some discernment and wisdom is needed in processing these requests. One way to handle this is to ask the pastors to write their prayer requests in a way that they would be comfortable with it being forwarded As Is.

Another way is for the prayer coordinator to be responsible for rewording these requests to reflect how to pray for the need, but not unnecessarily expose that leader by revealing private information. For example, if a pastor e-mails us and says they are really feeling burned out, the prayer request to other intercessors should not say, "Please pray for Pastor Sam because he is feeling very burned out!" A better way to communicate this need would be: "Let's agree for the Lord to refresh and strengthen Pastor Sam this next week." The key to rewording these prayer requests is to look at what is needed in the request and re-write the prayer request to reflect that need.

Pastors need to be able to be real with us without feeling like what they share will be broadcast in a negative light. This is how rumors get started and feelings get hurt. Maintaining confidentiality and how prayer requests are handled are key trust issues that must be in place for this kind of prayer shield to be utilized correctly. I always tell the intercessors that confidential information shared on the team can be discussed with those within the team, but not outside to others. Please be mindful that what is shared with an intercessor for the purpose of prayer should be considered a sacred trust. Our job as intercessors is always to guard, protect, and encourage those for whom we pray.

Coordinating Prayer Requests

When a pastoral prayer request comes in by e-mail, the coordinator then updates the intercessors. For each pastor, the coordinator has a distribution list of intercessors with their name entitled as the group name (for example, *P.Sam.INT* for Pastor Sam's designated intercession team). I usually have a copy of these distribution lists, in addition to the prayer coordinator, as a back up or if I need to communicate a prayer request directly to the teams. I like to stay in the loop partly, because I watch for patterns in the prayer requests. Watching for patterns helps me to gauge how the enemy may be attacking in a generalized sense so I can discern what the Lord may want to do on a larger scale of mobilizing prayer coverage involving other prayer teams. For example, if I see a significant pattern of health concerns, it may be a spiritual attack of infirmity targeting our leadership as well as the church.

I also like to be copied because this is also a tool I use to mentor someone who is new in coordinating the pastoral updates. I am usually copied both on the original e-mail that the pastors respond to as well as on the e-mail sent out to the designated pastoral prayer teams being activated. This way I can see what was originally communicated and how the requests were sent out by the coordinator. This is especially important when someone is being trained for this position.

Keeping Everyone in the Loop

Several of our pastors have ministry leaders that report directly to them who also have prayer requests. We have targeted a few of these leaders and included them in our distribution list for the pastoral updates. We cannot do this for every ministry leader, but there are a few that are necessary. Most of the ministry leaders should be in contact with their overseeing pastor for any personal prayer needs in addition to having home fellowship groups that can handle those requests. Those few we have included are usually paid staff members and I have asked these leaders to be sure to copy their overseeing pastor whenever they send us a prayer request. This way the communication lines remain clear and unified.

Emergency Prayer Mobilization

Prayer requests warranting emergency prayer mobilization should be for reasons like: car accidents, emergency surgeries, serious illnesses or injuries, and anything that may constitute immediate danger or physical harm. Most emergency situations are those things that need immediate prayer activation; I reserve this kind of prayer mobilization for these rare situations.

Currently, we have ten prayer teams totaling approximately 150 people. The prayer ministry is organized so that I can contact each prayer leader by e-mail and in turn have them update their teams with any church-wide prayer initiative or emergency prayer request when necessary. I did discover one flaw in this system one year when I received a call that our senior pastor was in the emergency room and in great physical pain. Although the e-mail system is good, in this case, I did not have time to wait for the intercessors to read their e-mail, we needed to mobilize prayer immediately! Through this experience, I have added a calling tree to our tools of communication. Recently, we had another situation where I needed to mobilize prayer very quickly, so in addition to sending an e-mail to the prayer leaders, I activated the calling tree as well. I am pleased to say that this has worked very effectively for us.

Calling Tree

The way the calling tree works begins with a phone call from me to one of the prayer ministry leaders. This activates the other prayer ministry leaders. Each of the prayer leaders have a calling tree for their own team which is then activated. This way I only need to make one or two calls at the most and everyone will be notified. All of the prayer leaders have a calling tree schematic with home and cell phone numbers listed and are familiar with who they need to contact when this is activated. We update this calling tree yearly at our January prayer leadership meeting or as needed. The prayer leaders also know that if they are not able to reach the person they are assigned to call that they need to leave a message and then continue to contact the next person on the calling tree until they speak with a live person. If for some reason I am on vacation or cannot be reached in an emergency situation, I have designated someone as my primary back-up in activating our prayer teams. If for some reason no one can be reached, the prayer ministry leaders know to activate the emergency calling tree. I have found utilizing a calling tree in addition to e-mail updates to be an incredibly effective method during those rare emergency situations.

Important Back-up Plans

Part of how the infrastructure is designed for our prayer teams is to never be dependent on any one person or leader in maintaining prayer coverage. I have tried hard to keep this plan simple, do-able, and with back-up plans in case a prayer leader is out of town or not available. One of these back-up plans includes every prayer leader having an assistant, familiar with all the functions of that prayer team, who can step in to lead if necessary. A few years ago, we did have a prayer leader need to take an emergency sabbatical due to a family crisis. She was out for about eight months. Fortunately, we had an assistant in place who was able to effectively step in and run the team. My purpose in organizing the prayer teams this way is so that prayer coverage is on-going regardless of whoever comes, goes, or when an emergency situation arises.

Personal Ministry Times

Since the prophetic intercession team is the primary team to pray over the church vision as well as keep our pastoral team covered in prayer, another way that I have utilized this team has been to invite our pastoral team to our team meeting if they would like to receive personal prayer. We have done this in a couple of different ways. One year, I was sensing that the Lord wanted to bring a refreshing to the pastoral staff, so we invited the pastors to one of our homes and had a night of ministry. We began with snacks and fellowship and then spent some time in praise and worship. Afterward, we organized into ministry teams. We had five teams of two or three intercessors praying prophetically over each pastor and their spouse. Each couple was ministered to for fifteen to twenty minutes. During our twenty minute cycle, whichever couple was not receiving prayer would take notes for the other couple by writing down any prophetic words articulated during the prayer time. The notes are not intended to be complete, but just general themes or key words jotted down to help people remember what was spoken later. Usually I will facilitate these the ministry times by keeping track of the time and transitioning everyone into the next twenty minute cycle. Between transitions, I will float amongst the ministry teams and prophesy to whoever is being ministered to.

We have set up an open door policy with our pastoral staff that they are always welcome to attend one of our prayer meetings where we will take time then to minister prophetically over them as a team. When one of the pastors comes we arrange it so that they can come for a portion of our meeting and leave when we are finished praying for them. On average, we spend about thirty to forty-five minutes praying for them. When they come I give them the option to either share some prayer needs before we pray or to just have us pray how the Holy Spirit directs us. Prophetic intercessors are very sensitive to the Spirit and can discern the direction of how to pray whether a prayer need has been communicated or not. So it really doesn't matter which way we begin.

Apostolic Prayer Shield

In our church, we have a founding pastor who ministers apostolically and travels quite extensively internationally. For his prayer shield we have an estimated thirty-five to forty prayer warriors constantly fasting and interceding for this apostolic ministry. Like the pastoral prayer shield, everyone on this shield is asked to fast one day a week and we have this organized so that all the days of the week are covered. This team also has a list of things to be praying in between prayer updates. I have a separate prayer coordinator who keeps abreast on our apostle's travel schedule and ministry focuses. The intercessors are updated every three weeks or so with prayer points for their general health, travel and connections, ministry effectiveness, times and places of ministry, refreshment, and anything else our apostle requests prayer for.

Senior Pastor Prayer Shield

For this prayer shield I mobilize all of the Prophetic Intercession Team as well as other prayer warriors in the church, who combined, make up about thirty people who are part of this prayer shield. Our pastoral prayer coordinator takes care of these updates while pastor is in town. When our senior pastor travels, I mobilize prayer coverage for him a little differently. Depending on where he is traveling, I try to gauge how much and what kind of prayer coverage is needed. When he travels internationally, I will usually have our Prophetic Intercession Team pray during one of our meetings for the ministry trip a few days before he goes. This really helps us to discern any kind of warfare that we need to be aware of as well as any prophetic sense of how the Lord wants to move through our pastor as he ministers. Our focus during this kind of prayer is to prepare the spiritual atmosphere for a greater receptivity for all that God desires to impart through our pastor in the delivery of the Word, leadership training, counseling, and throughout the ministry time. We believe that when the Lord gives either our apostle or our senior pastor an assignment, there is a deposit God has put within them to release over that city or nation and this deposit has the potential to bring transformation into people's lives in advancing the kingdom. So we spend time in prayer discerning and agreeing with what God desires to accomplish in the sending of His servants.

Usually I try to connect with my pastor about what the Lord has put on his heart concerning the ministry trip and weave this together with what our prophetic intercessors have discerned. Then I ask the Lord to help me pin point the important prayer focuses that reflects the prophetic theme of what the Lord desires to accomplish in this journey. With this in mind, I will write prayer declarations for our teams to be praying in agreement with while pastor is away ministering.

For some ministry trips, I will mobilize all the prayer teams as well as the prayer warriors who attend our weekly corporate prayer time. Sometimes, I just activate our senior pastor's team of personal intercessors and this automatically includes the prophetic intercession team. Other times I have organized a church-wide fast and put together prayer points to encourage more prayer participation and coverage. There is a variety of ways that I will activate prayer depending on what I am discerning is necessary.

While our pastor is traveling, he usually will update the intercessors via e-mail concerning how things are progressing. These updates are so life-giving to the intercessors. It helps them to feel a part of what is happening and that their prayers are making a difference as well as appreciated. Pastor is good at letting us know the breakthroughs he is experiencing as well as any challenges he's facing. Sometimes he sends these updates for me to forward and other times he will send an e-mail directly to all his personal intercessors. Maintaining regular communication during these kinds of ministry trips is very helpful in fine tuning how we can best target our prayers.

In Conclusion

In this chapter, I have attempted to explain the importance of keeping the pastoral staff in prayer, how to set up a prayer shield and what kinds of things to keep in mind as you pray, the proper way to administrate and articulate confidential prayer requests, understanding the criteria for emergency prayer needs, and how to mobilize prayer coverage for the varying needs of the pastoral staff. The early church understood that prayer *had* to be continuous because their warfare was continuous.

"But we will give ourselves continually to prayer and the ministry of the word."   *Acts 6:4*

Like the early church, if we want to see the gospel advance we must understand that engaging in prayer for our leaders is vital to this kingdom advancement.

The Role of a Watchman

"I have set watchmen on your walls, O Jerusalem; they shall never hold their peace day or night. You who make mention of the Lord, do not keep silent, and give him no rest till He establishes and till He makes Jerusalem a praise in the earth."

Isaiah 62:6-7

Defining Terms

The word used for *watchman* in this passage is from the Hebrew word *Shamar*. It means to keep guard, watch, or protect. *Shamar* has been used in scripture to describe watching over a garden[95], a flock[96], a house[97], the commandments of God[98], a promise[99], a person[100], and to watch over a city like a prophet[101]. This word also expresses the careful attention given to the conditions of God's covenant with Israel. All of these are important aspects that define the kind of assignments that God gives to those who are called to keep watch.

---

[95] Genesis 2:15
[96] Genesis 30:31
[97] Ecclesiastes 12:3
[98] 1 Kings 11:10
[99] 1 Kings 8:24-26
[100] 1 Samuel 26:15-16
[101] Isaiah 21:11; Isaiah 62:6

In Isaiah 62, the exhortation to the watchmen is a call to prayer over something that God has promised Israel. They are told not to keep silent, but to continue to remind the Lord of His promise until that word has been fulfilled. It is also clear from this passage that God places watchmen in their position. In this case, they are strategically placed on the walls of Jerusalem.

The fact that they are placed in an elevated position along the city walls is significant. It is from this vantage point that the watchman can discern the spiritual activity in three spheres: 1) what is happening inside the walls of the city or church, 2) outside the walls which has to do with where the city or church is situated within the region, and 3) what God is doing in the heavenly places. This is a good picture of how the role of the watchman functions today.

One truly called and appointed by the Lord to keep watch has a heightened ability to see and discern the spiritual activity over their assigned watch (that is, a church, a region, and even a nation). In Isaiah 62, it is clear that watchmen have watches that cover both day and nighttime hours. This means part of the watching assignment includes when and how long to watch. If you find yourself waking up at a certain time each night with a burden to pray; this may be the Lord prompting you to an assignment to watch and pray.

In the New Testament, there were watches to cover the evening, at midnight, at the crowing of the rooster and in the morning[102]. If you sense that you have been given a certain period of time to keep watch, be sure to ask the Lord what he is requiring of you to do in that specific time frame. He may prompt you to intercede, worship, make prophetic declarations, fast, read the Word or give you revelation. If you are not sure how to pray, you can always pray in tongues.

The Assignment of the Watchman

"Unless the Lord builds the house, they labor in vain who build it; unless the Lord guards the city, the watchman stays awake in vain."   *Psalm 127:1*

The important concept to grasp here is that watchman can only stand guard over what God himself is guarding. Otherwise there will be no fruit or victory in the ministry of the watchman. This is why Jesus says, "*Most assuredly, I say to you, the Son can do nothing of himself, but what He sees the Father do; for whatever He does, the son does in like manner." John 5:19.* Jesus is teaching us an important pattern here for effective ministry -- to discern what the Father is doing and follow suit. This is particularly true for the watchman. To be effective in their call, they must be careful to watch over those things that God has initiated.

---

[102] Mark 14:35

We can see from Psalm 127 that there is a potential for the ministry of the watchman to be in vain, this is the reason for the caution. Just because we have the prophetic gifts to be able to keep watch does not mean that we are correctly aligned with what the Father is doing. This is a sobering word. It reminds us to be careful that our assignments are God-initiated and not just a nice idea.

God wants to partner with the watchman in accomplishing His purposes in the earth. The scriptures are also clear that it is the Lord who appoints watchmen and it is He who assigns them to their watch. How does this happen? God will place His burden on your heart to pray over a certain matter. We respond by keeping that burden in prayer until the burden lifts or we can see an answer to that prayer.

"Then the Lord said to me, 'You have seen well, for I am ready to perform My word." Jeremiah 1:12

One of the nuggets we glean from Jeremiah is the nature of how God is ready to perform His word. The word *ready* is the Hebrew word *Shaqad.* In essence, it means to watch over carefully, in anticipation, for the appointed time or opportunity to fulfill His word. It also reveals God's heart in keeping watch and how He is monitoring the time and circumstances in fulfilling His word. It is significant that Jeremiah's eyes were opened to see prophetically into the spiritual realm what God was about to perform. This is how God partners with us as watchmen, prophets, and prophetic intercessors. He reveals his heart over a matter by activating the prophetic gifts in the form of visions, dreams, prophecy, and impressions so that we can then declare and pray agreement with the fulfillment of the word sent.

In the local church, the role of the watchman is to guard and protect in prayer, what has been articulated as the direction of the overall church vision. This includes the ministries associated with that vision such as: Children's ministry, Youth Ministry, Compassion Outreaches, Home fellowships, Music Ministry, and Prayer Ministry.

As we know from the Hebrew definition of the word *shamar*, the nature of a watchman is to guard and protect the forward movement of God's kingdom purposes in the earth. The assignment is to pray protection against any spiritual opposition. Why do we need to pray protection? Let's look at the Parable of the Sower:

"When anyone hears the word of the kingdom, and does not understand it, then the wicked one comes and snatches away what was sown into his heart. This is he who received the seed by the wayside. But he who received the seed on stony places, this is he who hears the word and immediately receives it with joy; yet he has no root in himself, but endures only for a while. For when tribulation or persecution arises because of the word, immediately he stumbles. Now he who received seed among the thorns is he who hears the word, and the cares of this world

and the deceitfulness of riches choke out the word, and he becomes unfruitful."   Matthew 13:19-22

We can see that the enemy wants to snatch the word before it is firmly established and produces fruit. Those particularly vulnerable to this attack are people who 1) lack a mature biblical understanding or foundation, 2) allow the pressures and care of the world to choke out the word, or 3) are not yet firmly established in applying faith to the word. Because we have a very real enemy who seeks to steal, kill, and destroy God's purposes in our lives, there is a need to be watchful.

If we refer back to Isaiah 62 for a moment, the picture we see is Israel in the process of restoration. Because of the spiritual opposition, the Lord exhorts the watchmen to continue to lay hold of the promise of God by praying and interceding until the word of restoration has been fulfilled. We do this by mixing our faith with His promise; we speak agreement with what he has declared. This is how we are called to war with the promises God has given us through His word!

Watchmen are called to War!

"Set up the standard on the walls of Babylon; Make the guard strong, set up the watchmen, prepare the ambushes. For the Lord has both devised and done what he has spoken against the inhabitants of Babylon."   Jeremiah 51:12

When the Lord executes judgment in the earth, as in the case of Babylon, he calls some things to be set in order to prepare for this kind of warfare. God calls the *standard*, or the battle flag, to be raised against Babylon as a signal that He is about to move. He calls for a refortifying of the guard and a setting in place of the watchmen. The reason for this is answered: *"For the Lord has both devised and done what he has spoken against the inhabitants of Babylon."* This means God is getting ready to fulfill a prophecy issued years before. In fulfilling this word, there are things God has prepared and ambushes that He will release, in this case against Babylon, at the appointed time. God has determined that the guard and the watchmen be strategically positioned in the execution of His word because of their ability to watch, defend, and war effectively.

Watchmen are also called to Warn!

"Son of man I have made you a watchman for the house of Israel; therefore hear a word from my mouth, and give them warning from me."   *Ezekiel 3:17*

God is expanding Ezekiel's call as a prophet to include being a watchman over the house of Israel. Very specific instructions were given to Ezekiel because of the condition of Israel at the time of this commissioning. He is exhorted to hear the Word of the Lord and then declare a warning to Israel. There are times when the watchman will have to issue a warning. In this situation, it was due to the spiritual condition of Israel. According to Ezekiel 3, watchmen are held accountable to issue a warning and to deliver God's message.

"When I say to the wicked, 'You shall surely die,' and you give him no warning, nor speak to warn the wicked of his way, to save his life, that same wicked man shall die in his iniquity; but his blood I will require at your hand. Yet, if you warn the wicked, and he does not turn from his wickedness, nor his wicked way, he shall surely die in his iniquity; but you have delivered your soul."   *Ezekiel 3:18-19*

The same is true when issuing a warning to the righteous that have deviated from God's path and are in sin. The watchman has the responsibility to deliver the warning[103] even if it is not received. A warning is both an opportunity for repentance as well as call to accountability. God's heart is to give every opportunity for a person whose way is unrighteous to repent. This further emphasizes the importance of being a good steward of the word that God has entrusted to you to speak.

The watchman is also able to discern the approach of messengers bringing good news.

"Now David was sitting between the two gates. And watchman went up to the roof over the gate, to the wall, lifted his eyes and looked, and there was a man running alone. Then the watchman cried out and told the king. And the king said, 'If he is alone, there is news in his mouth.' And he came rapidly and drew near. Then the watchman saw another man running, and the watchman called to the gatekeeper and said, 'There is

---

[103] Ezekiel 33:3-6

another man running alone!' And the king said, 'He also brings news.' So the watchman said, 'I think the running of the first is like the running of Ahimaaz the son of Zadok.' And the king said, 'He is a good man, and comes with good news."

2 Samuel 18:24-27

There is an interesting relationship between the king and the watchman in this passage. The king is depending on the acuity of the watchman's vision to know what is approaching the city gates. The watchman notices the running patterns of the messenger and recognizes this pattern of movement to be like that of Ahimaaz, the son of Zadok. As the watchman describes what he sees, the king is given further wisdom about the nature of the approaching messengers. As they discuss the situation, there is a synergy between them that releases further wisdom in accurately discerning the situation. It is important to see how the watchman and the King needed each other to discern a complete picture of what was approaching. Based on that discernment, the King would have to decide whether or not to open the city gates. This is similar to how prophetic intercessors or watchmen are to flow together with a senior pastor or an apostle. The watchman has the ability to recognize familiar patterns of how the Holy Spirit is moving as well as demonic activity. The communication between a senior pastor/apostle and a watchman will often ignite further revelation and strategies concerning the spiritual climate surrounding the regional or local church. It is this kind of regular communication, discernment, and partnering that serves as an important key in seeing effective ministry take place and the kingdom advance.

Characteristics of the Watchman

Prophetic intercessors, called to be watchmen, are intensely loyal and faithful. Like the Roman centurion in the New Testament, a watchman is a strong warrior who has an innate understanding of spiritual authority. As a result they take their spiritual assignments very seriously.

I have noticed that watchmen also serve with an attitude of humility, submission, and respect. They have a genuine love and care for those leaders they support. They are also spiritually alert, watchful, and often receive strategies to skillfully defend in prayer those they are called to watch. Watchmen have an on-going prophetic sense of the spiritual climate over people, churches, and regions. They do not seek recognition or honor, but rather find great joy in seeing the purposes of God fully released in churches, regions, nations, and over the lives of leaders they are assigned to keep in prayer.

What Does the Watchman Watch For?

The primary function of a watchman is to continue to pray agreement with a word God has declared through His prophets, until His Word is fulfilled[104]. In doing so, the watchman also is positioned to keep watch over the spiritual climate surrounding this Word. If the prophecy has to do with the local church, then the watchman keeps watch by discerning three things:

1) How the Holy Spirit is moving so they can come into agreement.

2) How there may be demonic opposition opposing the work of God from advancing.

3) How the Lord would have them counter any spiritual attack.

What are the types of spiritual attacks to be on alert for? I watch for patterns among the body of Christ such as people experiencing things such as illness, weariness, hopelessness, discouragement, fear, heaviness, the loss of employment, miscommunications, broken relationships (friendships, ministry, marriage, and family), accidents, confusion, distractions, lack of direction and purpose, and division impacting the body of Christ. When you see a significant pattern of people experiencing the same kinds of things, this is an indicator of the demonic opposition that may be targeting the body of Christ.

What is the reason for these kinds of attacks? There are a few reasons—all have to do with the vision and calling over God's people. The enemy cannot stop the purposes of God, so instead he throws obstacles at the body of Christ in an attempt

---

[104] Isaiah 62:6-7

to render it ineffective. At the core of what opposes us the most is a strategy to challenge our faith in God. So the devil stirs up situations to cause fear and unbelief. He tempts us to see our circumstances as greater than God's ability to overcome. This form of unbelief throws up a roadblock that, in essence, moves us out of our position of faith in God which moves us forward in accomplishing kingdom purposes. Satan ultimately wants our attention and focus; he wants us to give in to our carnal nature. In the book of James, we learn how our carnal nature desires to rule us. When we give in to our flesh, it creates in us a vulnerability for the enemy to establish a legal right to harass us until we repent.

To illustrate this point, let's revisit James 3 for a moment.

"For jealousy and selfishness are not God's kind of wisdom. Such things are earthly, unspiritual, and motivated by the devil. For where there is jealousy and selfish ambition, there you will find disorder and every kind of evil." James 3:15-16 (NLT)

This is what is meant by *"where you find jealousy and selfish ambition, there you will find disorder and every kind of evil."* Our carnal nature opens the door to disorder and every kind of evil. On the flip side of these attacks, God also wants to deal with our character. Even though the Lord does not send these attacks, He will allow them to test and refine our faith. Our position as watchmen is to discern and agree with God's heart concerning a matter.

This is where the prophetic gifts play a key role in enabling the watchman to keep watch. Like the prophetic intercessor, the word of wisdom, word of knowledge, discernment of spirits, and prophecy are the spiritual gifts which empower the watchman to see, hear, and discern the spiritual climate. As we have been discussing, the type of intercessor that flows in these revelation gifts has been identified as a prophetic intercessor. Just because someone is a prophetic intercessor does not necessarily mean they are also called to be a watchman. The difference has to do with the prayer burden God has given them and their ability to watch and pray for a local church, city, region or nation. I believe there can be several assignments within a watchman's calling. Some may find their primary prayer burden is for the in the local church. Others may discern on a regional, state or national level. Others are able to discern on multiple levels.

In praying over the vision of your local church, let's review some things to keep in mind, pay attention to the direction the senior pastor is leading the church. Remember, like prophetic intercessors, watchmen are not responsible for setting the future direction of the church, but to cover in prayer the vision already established. If you are in a recognized five-fold ministry role of a prophet or a pastor in addition to having a prophetic intercessory gift, then you have a unique dual role as it relates to speaking into the forward direction of the church. For most of the prophetic intercessors reading this book where this is not the case, once the church vision is given to the body of Christ, the watchman watches and prays.

As previously mentioned, it is important to pay attention to what has been said prophetically over the church by the leadership as well as any visiting apostles or prophets. I have found it very helpful to keep a running record of prophetic words that come forth during our church services. If the services are taped, then have one of the intercessors transcribe them and keep these in a binder for reference. This will help to keep these prophetic words covered in prayer and fresh in our minds.

So what does the watchman watch for? The watchman discerns the movement and presence of God as well as any spiritual attack or hindrance of the enemy. Often times this discernment comes simultaneously. Remember the devil is a master in attempting to shift our attention on him. So it is important to keep our eyes on the Lord and focus our attention on His purposes. It is so easy to focus on the enemy and ignore the flow of the Holy Spirit. This is where we run the risk of becoming reactionary by engaging in spiritual warfare solely because of what we see the enemy doing. Discerning demonic activity is only part of the picture; the other part is sensing how the Holy Spirit desires to move. One thing we must never do in warfare is to react hastily when we discern the enemy's movement. In other words, do not allow the enemy to dictate when to engage in spiritual warfare; not every battle is for us to fight. There are battles where the instruction of the Lord is to "*stand still and see the salvation of the Lord* [105]" because the Lord is taking up the battle Himself.

"The Lord will fight for you, and you shall hold your peace."

Exodus 14:14

When you discern demonic activity, stop and pause to inquire of the Lord of how you are to respond to the warfare you discern. Keep in mind that it is not always necessary to rebuke the enemy if you know what the Lord is saying in a situation. Agreeing with the Lord over His revealed direction often times takes care of demonic opposition. When we pray in agreement with a true prophetic word we are also aligning with what God desires to be accomplished in the earth.

On a prayer team, the prayer leader has a unique responsibility to discern the prophetic theme of what God has been generally speaking over the church; from this thread you can set a couple of prayer points to focus on during the prayer meeting. Discerning this prophetic thread is also an important aspect of activating the revelation gifts in prayer. When we touch on areas that are on God's heart, there is an immediate release of the prophetic anointing upon the intercessory team to enter into prophetic intercession. It is like when you plug a lamp into the wall and the light immediately comes on. Usually we can see many areas needing prayer, but the key is to discern what is on the Father's heart. Once this happens, the revelation gifts are

---

[105] Exodus 14:13

activated and the intercessors begin receiving prophetic insight through a vision, Rhema Words, an impression, or prophecy. The prayer leader will usually discern how to mobilize the team to pray through the revelation that is shared.

The Watchman Role during Church Services

During a church service it is important to be on watch. I usually ask our prophetic intercessors to be on alert as they are sitting in the congregation. What are they watching for? They watch for any demonic activity trying to distract or hinder God's purposes for that service. Especially if anything unusual is happening like sound system and multimedia difficulties, fire alarms going off, or if the speaker is having difficulty articulating thoughts. Our pastor is extremely articulate, so if I notice him having trouble articulating his thoughts, concentrating, losing his place in the message, or appear to be a little confused, this is an indicator that he may be experiencing some spiritual opposition. If a speaker ever stops mid-message and says, "Let's just stop a minute and pray." That is a very graceful way of saying, "I'm experiencing some warfare concerning the message and need prayer in breaking through." Although the congregation will already have prayed a prayer of agreement with the speaker, intercessors should continue to stay alert and praying.

We also watch for difficulties in pressing through to God's presence during praise and worship. The prophetic gifts help to identify what kind of opposition is manifesting (that is, distractions, a spirit of heaviness, hindering spirits, witchcraft).

Sometimes people come to church with relational and financial burdens weighing them down so much that it is difficult to concentrate. Usually when an intercessor discerns this kind of weight or distraction, it is because a significant number of people have come to church feeling the same kind of burden and it is impacting the atmosphere. The prophetic intercessor should then ask the Lord how to respond. The Holy Spirit may lead that intercessor to bind and rebuke the spirit of heaviness, or declare a countering scripture such as Matthew 11:30, *"For my yoke is easy and My burden is light."* The intercessor may pray the opposite of what is manifesting, or pray agreement with how the Holy Spirit is moving in the service.

On rare occasions we have discerned people who are heavily involved in occult practices (Wicca, Satanism, New Age, and so on). When we sense this, many times the Lord may even show us specifically who it is, so we pray for their salvation, plead the blood of Jesus, and ask the Lord to minister to them. We also pray that the Lord would remove them if they intend to bring harm to the body by releasing curses or by intentionally leading others astray. Usually, if they are not open to the Lord, they become uncomfortable and leave.

In Conclusion

The watchman, in the local church, is an intercessory role designed to protect the forward movement of the church vision as articulated by the church leadership. In this chapter, we have discussed how the revelation gifts help us to keep watch, what to be on alert for, and what to do with what we see. We have also explored the attributes of prophetic intercessors called to be watchmen as well as how the Lord appoints the watchmen to their assignment. We have explored the various ways of how a watchman may be used in keeping watch. Lastly, we have discussed the importance of the connection between the watchman and their pastor or apostolic leader brings a more complete picture of what God is revealing; especially in how to secure victory in the advancement of God's kingdom purposes in the earth.

"Watch and pray, lest you enter into temptation. The spirit is indeed willing, but the flesh is weak."   Matthew 26:41

Kingdom Advancement and the Benefit

of

Prophetic Intercession

"The earnest prayer of a righteous person has great power and
wonderful results"   *James 5:16b (NLT)*

Kingdom advancement has to do with God's transforming power and presence impacting geographical areas as well as individual lives. When God visits a region, all levels of society and the very land itself can be impacted. According to George Otis Junior's research, revival has broken out and whole communities have experienced a divine encounter with God in a growing number of places around the world. Evidence and testimonies from these encounters with God include reports of groups of people receiving salvation; healing and creative miracles have been experienced physically, emotionally and even economically; unjust laws and rulings have been overturned; and even the land itself has shown healing[106].

What causes this kind of transformation to occur? The first step is in recognizing that God has a redemptive purpose for people, cities, and nations. Activating God's plan for radical

---

[106] See Confronting the Powers by C.Peter Wagner p.217-222

transformation involves partnering with the Lord in prayer and engaging in prophetic intercession.

*"And He has made from one blood every nation of men to dwell on the face of the earth, and has determined their **pre-appointed times and the boundaries of their dwellings, so that they should Seek the Lord**, in the hope that they might grope for Him and find Him, though He is not far from each one of us."*

Acts 17:26-27

From this passage, we can see God has strategically placed people in their dwellings and in the most likely place that would cause them to seek the Lord. It shows that God purposed in His heart that our places of dwelling would hold a redemptive purpose! God's purpose includes a special grace upon the land and the people groups associated with each geographical area that can cause a further release of God's plan to spread the salvation message to all of mankind. As the Body of Christ, we are His means to spread the good news of salvation through Jesus Christ. That is why God has empowered His church with various spiritual gifts and special graces to accomplish this task. Through God's plan we have been specially designed as differing, yet necessary, parts of the Body of Christ to function together in fulfilling this great commission.

"And He said to them, Go into all the world and preach the gospel to every creature. He who believes and is baptized will be saved; but he who does not believe will be condemned."
Mark 16:15-16

Because of this command to preach the gospel to the world, we must also understand that all spiritual opposition aims to stop the advancement of the gospel. This is true on several different levels. On one level, the devil attacks the church. If he can divide us through various offenses, we are not a united force in our advance. On another level, the devil attacks individual Christians to try to frustrate or derail the divine calling on our lives. We must realize each of us is given an important part to play in the Body of Christ that is part of a greater plan to reach the lost. We also need to be aware of how this plan is simply carried out in our everyday lives each time we choose to reflect Christ in our words or actions to others. As we allow the light of Christ to shine through us, it has an impact on the spiritual environment around us. Another level of spiritual attack is in the lives of those who are lost.

"But even if our gospel is veiled, it is veiled to those who are perishing, whose minds the god of this age has blinded, who do not believe, lest the light of the glory of Christ , who is the image of God, should shine on them."   *2 Corinthians 4:4*

The devil holds nonbelievers in a place of spiritual blindness and deception, so they are unable to receive the truth of the salvation message. Fortunately, Jesus made a provision for the church to counter this demonic opposition so that His church would not be left helpless in fulfilling His command to go into all the world.

"Having disarmed principalities and powers, He made a public spectacle of them, triumphing over them in it." Colossians 2:15

The book of Colossians makes it very clear that, through the transforming work of the cross, all principalities and powers have been stripped of their power. Because Jesus has triumphed over the powers of darkness, we can now exercise our spiritual gifts, authority in Christ, and prayer to appropriate healing and deliverance for a lost and dying world. The true nature of our warfare mainly is in appropriating what Jesus has already accomplished for us at Calvary. In this context we can appreciate how prophetic gifts can help advance the gospel message and impact our communities.

Prophetic intercession can help the church to strategically advance when we work with our church leaders to discern what God wants to accomplish through our prayers. This collaboration is especially important to the vision God has given to the leaders of a local or regional church.

Prophetic intercessors are like the reconnaissance forces sent by the military to carry out secret missions behind enemy lines. Often the goal of our assignments is to gather spiritual intelligence so that we can execute our mission with greater effectiveness. When prophetic intercessors receive prophetic insight or spiritual discernment, they are gaining a heavenly perspective about how to wage war effectively. As they pray in agreement with God's revealed plan, God then moves on behalf of those prayers and creates a place in the earthly realm to fulfill His declared word or promise. Prophetic prayer agreement with God's will can be a tremendous support to church leaders as they lead the advance of the vision God has given to them.

"Blessed be the Lord my strength, who teaches my hands to war, and my fingers to fight." Psalm 144:1

In Psalm 144 we learn that when we rely on God's strength, as we seek Him in prayer, the Lord instructs us how to battle and when to engage. *Hands* in this passage are a figurative description of God's enabling strength to bring about deliverance, and *fingers* have to do with skill. So, David is revealing how our dependence upon God releases His enabling strength and wisdom to fight effectively in spiritual warfare. This is also a great picture of how prophetic intercession works. As we learn to listen and rely on His instruction rather than our own understanding, the Lord then supernaturally reveals strategies to increase our skill in securing victory.

One of the main benefits of a prophetic prayer team is that the revelation gifts create a synergy within the team as they enter into a prophetic prayer flow. The prophetic insight of the group allows the team to perceive what God is revealing about a matter with a greater depth and perspective. With a greater sense of prophetic insight, they can target their prayers more precisely.

When intercessors are given discernment and prophetic insight, it often allows them to discern the spiritual atmosphere over people, places, and geographical areas. The discernment of spirits especially serves as a protection for the local and regional church. Through God's revelation, demonic activity is exposed and spiritual strongholds that hinder the advance of the local and regional church can be identified and dismantled. Strongholds are systems of demonically inspired lies that people believe as truth.

Strongholds are dismantled when the authority of Christ and His word are applied to an area of darkness that has held people in bondage. Christ's authority can affect people groups within a geographical area as well as individuals. Dismantling a stronghold involves breaking agreement with these thought patterns by asking God for forgiveness wherever we agreed with lies and by rebuking the demonic influence causing these thoughts. Evil spirits must then yield to the authority of Jesus Christ. Also, the skilled use of God's Word (*logos*) when it is applied to a particular situation or circumstance can separate truth from error and free those caught in the enemy's grip.

"For the word of God is living and powerful, and sharper than any two-edged sword, piercing even to the division of soul and spirit, and of joints and marrow, and is a discerner of the thoughts and intents of the heart."　　　　*Hebrews 4:12*

The authority we have been given in Christ and the application of His Word are part of the necessary arsenal to dismantle demonic strongholds and ungodly belief systems. Prophetic intercession simply helps to pinpoint where the application of the Word needs to be made. Strategic prayers can be useful not only to loosen the enemy's influence, but also to establish a spiritual hedge of protection that lets the church advance in effective ministry.

When prophetic and general intercessors engage in spiritual warfare, the spiritual atmosphere is significantly changed. Effective *warfare prayer* establishes spiritual boundaries that limit or stop demonic opposition from influencing a person, situation, or geographical area. Warfare prayer clears the atmosphere so God's kingdom can move forward. It is similar to the way a farmer tills a field before planting seeds. The farmer prepares the soil so that the crop will be unhindered in its growth for that season. The same principle applies in prayer.

The evidence of effective intercession is revealed by the changes in people's lives. Intercession is effective when we notice the lost are more open to receive the gospel, the messages preached in church services have a greater impact in changing lives, the presence of God is more tangible, and people experience physical healing, deliverance, and miracles. Also, there even seems to be an ease to ministry.

It is my personal belief that God has designed pastors and prophetic intercessors to work together in the Body of Christ to discern the spiritual atmosphere and God's strategies to accomplish God's kingdom purposes. Pastors are given a different level of spiritual discernment for their call to watch over the flock as well as to receive the vision for how a particular local church is called to advance.

As pastors and intercessors work together, there should be a strong agreement about what they are hearing from the Lord. Connecting effectively involves choosing a time to pray together and then choosing a time to discuss prophetic insights. Prophetic intercessors can add valuable insight to confirm the accuracy of what the leaders are discerning. God has equipped prophetic intercessors as the part of the army stationed along the wall to observe spiritual activity. When church leaders and prophetic intercessors work together, there is a tremendous synergy that affects the ability of the church members to move forward together and fulfill their part of the great commission.

If you are a pastor looking for a starting point to develop prayer and prophetic intercession in your congregation, I would like to encourage you to first create a culture of prayer within your local church. A culture of prayer has to do with imparting the value of prayer to all church members and not just designating prayer to the faithful few. For ministry to truly be effective, we must realize that we are all called to pray as the Apostle Paul exhorts us in 1 Timothy 2:1-2:

"I exhort therefore, that first of all, supplications, prayers, intercessions, and giving of thanks, be made for all men, for kings and all who are in authority that we may lead a quiet and peaceable life in all godliness and reverence."

A great place to begin this process is by developing a corporate prayer time in which the church leaders are committed to attending regularly. It is vital that the value of prayer be imparted to the whole church. The best way to show the value of prayer is by the church leaders serving as primary role models. Allow time for prayer to be integrated as an essential part of every ministry expression in your local church. When this is in place, then begin mobilizing the prophetic intercessors and developing other intercessory teams.

Peppered throughout most of your congregations are prophetic intercessors who are designed by God to support the church leadership and pray for the vision of the church. Do not feel that you need to understand everything about prophetic intercession before you connect with these intercessors. Chances are that they are still learning too! They need the rich deposit of God within you as much as you have need of them. Mutual interdependence is by God's design. If you already have a well-defined group of prophetic intercessors, then begin to connect with them regularly. Use this time to impart the vision of what the Lord has revealed to you and ask them to begin covering this vision in prayer.

One Final Thought

It is my personal conviction and experience that God does move mightily when pastors and prophetic intercessors are willing to submit themselves to a process of learning how to work together and draw strength from each other. It is a process in which we must be patient, but a process that yields much fruit in advancing the kingdom of God!

"If My people who are called by My name will humble themselves, and pray and seek My face, and turn from their wicked ways, then I will hear from heaven, and will forgive their sin and heal their land"   *2 Chronicles 7:14*

What a tremendous promise we have to see our cities and nations healed by the transforming power of God. The key to unlock this kind of transformation is PRAYER!

Afterword
by Dr. David Cannistraci

In *Advancing Kingdom Purposes Through Prophetic Intercession*, you have no doubt been energized with a revelation that will fuel your life as an intercessor. What was previously dim and dull has been illuminated with a fresh light, exposing another dimension of God's purpose in the church and in your life. The course has now been revealed, and the starting gun has been fired. The only question is: *Are you ready to run with the revelation?*

The Kingdom of God is meant to advance. But how does the Kingdom of God move forward through prophetic intercession? Through prophetic intercession...

1. *Christ's present plan* is accurately discerned

2. *Christ's people* come into agreement and precise alignment

3. *Christ's power* is released in a laser-like fashion against the structures of darkness

4. *Christ's presence* displaces the power of the enemy in people's lives, and

5. *Christ's purpose* expands and takes root in the earth.

I've seen each of these indispensable blessings operating in our church and in our city to one degree or another through the power of prophetic intercession. Our influence has been strengthened and advanced by practicing these life-giving truths. Now, it is your turn to see the Lord move you and your church forward.

What will you do with your calling as an intercessor? If you have not done so, I encourage you to get aligned with a strong pastor and take your place in the race. Don't let the enemy stop you in your pursuit of the calling to pray. Don't let your past hurts and frustrations block your path. Be healed as you begin to activate what you have learned here. Watch the purposes of God in you and through you advance in a new way.

If you are a pastor or a leader in the Body of Christ, *what will you do to release this prayer flow in your sphere of ministry?* If you are not already doing so, I encourage you to *love*, *lead* and *listen* to your prophetic intercessors. They are all around you, awaiting your blessing, affirmation and support.

Some leaders are afraid of intercessors. They've heard second-hand stories about intercessors being over-spiritual, controlling, oversensitive or weird. Other leaders downplay the importance of an intercessor's role. As a pastor for many years, I can assure you that both positions are a terrible mistake. While some intercessors have gone astray, a true intercessor longs to function properly and align squarely with God's Word and your God-given vision. I have learned that prophetic intercessors are irreplaceable in my life and ministry. I long for you to experience the same benefit.

You are done with the book, but you're just beginning your new race. It's time to pray. You are the one. Today is the day. God has called you. Go ahead—take the first step. I'll be looking for you at the finish line.

Ellen Laitinen

Appendix A

PROPHETIC GIFT SURVEY

Please place a check by only those statements that you clearly identify with. If there is one that you are not sure about, put a question mark by it. Do not feel concerned if you are only able to check off a few. This questionnaire is intended to help you identify any prophetic gift you may have.

_____1) Often sense how God wants to move in a church service and pray agreement.

_____2) I am able to distinguish what kind of demonic presence may be present (fear, heaviness, confusion etc…)

_____3) Can tell the difference between the spirit of God, the demonic and a human spirit behind the actions and words of others.

_____4) Often receive a strategy of how to pray specifically for a person or situation.

_____5) Experience a sudden knowing about a past, present, or future detail concerning people or situations you know nothing about.

_____6) Experience a sudden knowing of God's clear direction in how to pray.

_____7) I hear Words in my Spirit that I feel prompted to speak.

_____8) Have an impression during prayer of a word like "breakthrough" or "Joy" in relation to how God is working in someone's life.

_____9) Sometimes receive a message of what God wants to speak to a person or about a situation.

_____10) Have a heightened awareness of the spiritual climate in the atmosphere around me and other people.

_____11) I have given a prophecy and had it affirmed by the leadership.

_____12) In different situations, I can sense a demonic presence or a strong presence of the Lord.

Prophetic Gifts:

Word of Knowledge: 1   5   8

Word of Wisdom: 1   4   6

Discernment of Spirits: 2   3   10   12

Prophecy: 7   9   11

The results of this survey are designed to reveal indicators of any prophetic gifts. If you circled two or more in the above section, please place a check by that revelation gift.

____Word of Knowledge

____Word of Wisdom

____Discernment of Spirits

____Prophecy

Glossary of Terms

Glossary terms are defined according to the author's use of the term.

A

Accuser of the Brethren – A biblical reference to Satan as the one who stands before God accusing mankind.

Administrate – Has to do with the order of how a task is completed or handled.

Ambassadors – As Christians, we have been deputized as God's messengers of reconciliation between God and mankind.

Anointing – The spiritual empowerment, gift, or special grace given by God to complete a task or God-given assignment in regards to either the strengthening the Body of Christ or in reaching the lost with the gospel message.

Apostle – One who is sent by God to a people group. The spiritual gift of Apostle has to do with the spiritual authority exercised in the founding and oversight of local churches.

Apostolic People – Dr. David Cannistraci defines this as "Christians who support and participate in apostolic ministry, but who are not actual apostles."[107] One characteristic of an apostolic people is that they reflect the characteristics of the apostolic ministry they serve.

Appropriation – The act of utilizing a provision set aside for specific use. As Christians this has to do with every spiritual blessing, fruit, gift, and grace we have been given in Christ Jesus affecting our spiritual, physical and emotional restoration as well as the necessary spiritual weapons to overcome all

---

[107] See page 29 of *Apostles and the Emerging Apostolic Movement*

demonic opposition in fulfilling our destiny and calling in advancing the kingdom.

Armor Bearer – An intercessor with a prayer assignment to cover a specific person or leader.

Armor of God – The necessary spiritual armor outlined in Ephesians 6 that we must utilize to obtain victory in our spiritual battles.

B

Backsliders – Believers who have fallen away from living in accordance to the biblical truths of their salvation.

Belief Systems – Anything believed or accepted as true; belief systems are a source of guidance to how one behaves.

Binding and Loosing – Terminology used to describe utilizing a believer's spiritual authority to limit and break demonic bondages over people's lives.

Body of Christ – All those who embrace the gospel of Jesus Christ, are born again, and are considered part of the bride of Christ or the church.

Bondage – The condition of being enslaved by patterns of sin or addictions.

Breach – An opening or a gap made by breaking through or a weakening of what is other wise a place of strength and protection (that is, city walls, moral decline, sin, and injustices are places where societal and spiritual breaches can occur in individual lives as well as cities and nations).

C

Calvary – The location near Jerusalem where Jesus died; a reference to what Jesus accomplished at the cross on behalf of all mankind.

Charismatic Witchcraft – Deliberately praying your own will instead of God's for selfish reasons or personal gain; a form of manipulation.

Church Vision – The specific direction that God has revealed to a local church leadership in fulfilling their assignment in the great commission.

Control – In attempt to avoid hurt or pain, control is a defense mechanism by which one attempts to manipulate circumstances in order to obtain a particular outcome.

Corporate Prayer – A Church-wide prayer emphasis.

Culture of Prayer – Imparting the value of prayer to all church members and allowing this to permeate every ministry in the local church as a core value for experiencing effective ministry.

Curse – Calling on God or an evil spirit to bring harm or trouble on someone.

<u>D</u>

Deception – Believing in something of a false nature; to fool someone.

Declarations – A verbal announcement of the known will of God based on the truth revealed in scripture (logos), a Rhema word, or prophecy.

Deliverance – To set free from an evil influence or bondage as it impacts individual people and geographical areas.

Deliverance Ministry – A ministry designed to free individuals from generational sins, iniquities, and other demonic bondages.

Demons – Evil spirits with negative characteristics associated with Satan (that is, fear, anger, rebellion) who attempt to influence the behavior of mankind.

Demonic – Something of an evil or satanic nature.

Demonic Influence – An evil power prompting the actions of a person.

Demonic Realm – A reference to the hierarchy of the demonic and the arena in which they function (that is, principalities, powers, rulers of darkness, demons operating in the spirit world).

Demonic Strategies – Evil schemes devised or formulated by demons.

Diabolical Plan – A specific demonic scheme designed to oppose the purposes of God in fulfilling the great commission through individual believers or a local church body.

Discernment of Spirits – A spiritual gift with an ability to discern the difference between the Spirit of God, a demonic spirit, or the human spirit working within a situation.

Displacement – As a demonic spirit loses influence, the Spirit of God increases in strength over a geographic area.

Divine Opportunities/Appointments – An opportunity that opens as a result of a divine intervention or favor.

Divine Purposes – God's designed plans for what He desires to accomplish in the earth through our lives as well as through the body of Christ.

Dreams – God-inspired dreams are a vehicle by which God communicates a message to people.

Dry Season – A season where it does not appear to be anything of significance happening.

E

Edification – The process of building up or encouraging.

Evangelism – Sharing the gospel message with others.

Exhortation – An encouragement to someone in a certain direction of action or response.

F

Fiery Darts – A scriptural reference to demonic thoughts of doubt, unbelief, fear, discouragement, mocking and accusations that are aimed at believers with the intent to weaken faith or trust in God.

Fleshly Influence – Enticements of the world that appeal to our carnal nature as a way to influence a person toward ungodly behavior.

Foothold – A place of sin or a mindset that allows the devil to have a legal right to accuse, harass, or torment people.

G

Gap – See "Breach."

Generational Bondages – Patterns of sin or behavioral tendencies that can be passed down from parents to children extending over several generations (that is, physical abuse, mental illness alcoholism, rebellion, violence, theft).

Generational Blessings – Areas of graces, strengths, and virtues that can characterize a family line (that is, wealth, godliness and other spiritual virtues, musical abilities, leadership qualities, administrative abilities, writing abilities, favor and influence, intellectual ability, gifted in sports, hospitality, pastoral or missionary call).

Generational Curses – Areas of sin in a family's generational life that empowers a curse until the sin is dealt with or the curse is broken (that is, Types of curses: barrenness, sickness, poverty, pre-mature death, famine, vagabonism).

Generational Iniquities – Familial sin patterns; see "Generational Bondages."

Grace – A supernatural empowering of the Holy Spirit to accomplish a God-given assignment.

Ground-level warfare – Spiritual warfare that has to do with a lower ranking of demons (that is, fear, anger, infirmity) as opposed to more strategic levels of warfare (that is, churches, cities, or nations).

H

Heavenly Places – The atmosphere over geographical areas where principalities, powers and rulers of darkness illegally exercise their demonic influence over people groups. It's a place of conflict between angelic and demonic forces.

Hindrance/hindering spirit – Demonic opposition, experienced in the natural, to prevent forward movement in the accomplishing of an assignment or task.

Human Reasoning – Relying on ones own understanding or thought processes rather than God's.

I

Idolatry – Anything that is admired, loved, or worshipped more than God. A subtle form of idolatry can even be when we view our difficulties as greater than God's ability to provide, overcome or protect us.

Impartation – To leave a deposit of spiritual knowledge, wisdom, or grace to a person or a group of people that can then be embraced or utilized. It often comes through the laying on of hands through prayer (that is, to impart a blessing, spiritual gift, confirm a spiritual call).

Impression – Impressions are the effect of the Holy Spirit causing a prophetic thought to be impressed upon your spirit. Impressions are not as clear as dreams or visions; they are more a vague sensing of what the Lord is communicating.

Iniquity – Familial tendencies toward behavioral patterns of sin.

Injustice – Something experienced that is unjust or unfair.

Intercede – To seek God on behalf of another person, city, or nation.

Intercession – See "Intercede."

Intercessor – A person who seeks God on behalf of another person, city, or nation.

Intercessory Leader –A person designated by the church leadership to lead a prayer team.

Interdependent – Someone or something that is dependent on another in order to function.

Interrelate – Has to do with the necessity of connecting within a relational structure because of how closely things are connected and needing to work together for increased effectiveness (that is, churches, ministries, programs, businesses, etc.).

J

Jezebel – An Old Testament biblical character who was a wicked queen and whose negative character traits were known as manipulative, controlling, and seductive. (1 Kings 21:1-29) Also a known spiritual enemy opposing prophetic ministry (1Kings 18:4)

K

Kingdom advancement – Has to do with effective ministry. Ministry that a) strengthens the body of Christ, b) results in the spreading of the gospel to all of mankind and c) those in darkness experience salvation.

L

Leviathan – An Old Testament sea monster associated with the spirit of pride and division (Job 41:1-34).

Liaison – Someone who can serve as a connection between two groups of people.

Logos – Reference to the written word of God, the bible made up of 66 books with authors writing each book by the divine inspiration of the Holy Spirit.

M

Mandate – An order or a command issued by one in authority. A spiritual requirement given by God for all believers (that is, to love your neighbor as yourself, to pray for those in authority, to share the gospel message).

Manifestation – Something that is shown or revealed in words, actions, or in circumstances.

Manipulation – To control people or circumstances in an unjust way for personal gain.

N

Natural Realm –The physical reality of life as we know and experience it here on earth.

Natural Events – Occurrences that happen to mankind as part of our human existence.

Ellen Laitinen

O

Occult – Accessing spiritual knowledge or power outside of the Holy Spirit.

Offenses – Actions or words that may cause anger or hurt feelings in another person.

Oppression – A sense of feeling weighed down in your thoughts or emotions that may be a result of a demonic attack.

P

Pastoral Care – Care given by a pastor in the form of counseling or encouragement to those attending a local church.

Physical Manifestations (discernment) – Something revealed of a demonic nature or by the Holy Spirit that can be felt physically, seen, or rarely even heard.

Personal Intercessor – One who prays regularly for a particular person or leader.

Positional Authority – Authority that comes from occupying a leadership position. It also has to do with our spiritual inheritance and authority resulting from being co-heirs with Christ Jesus.

Power of Agreement – A union formulated between two or more individuals pertaining to a particular matter or promise.

Power – The strength or force, either demonic or by the Holy Spirit, by which something is done.

Powers of Darkness – Demonic spirits attempting to influence the behavior of people or groups of people through thoughts.

Praise and Worship – The portion of a church service when praise and the worship of God is expressed through music and songs.

Prayer – Seeking the mind of God about a matter or making a request to God about something needed or desired.

Prayer Assignment – A God-inspired burden to pray about a matter until there is a sense of release or the burden has lifted.

Prayer Burden – A God-inspired burden to pray about a particular person or situation.

Prayer Point – A specific prayer focus.

Proclamations – To declare something openly. In prayer, it is an authoritative verbal act which reinforces the will of God.

Prayer Shield – A term used to describe a team of intercessors with a specific prayer assignment to pray for the pastoral leadership team or individual leader, the church vision, or a particular outreach.

Prayer Strategies – A word of wisdom that reveals a specific way for something to be done.

Prayer Watch – A specific time of the day or night that the Lord has called an intercessor to watch and pray.

Prayer Warrior – One who feels a call and God-inspired burden to pray.

Principalities – A type of leader in the demonic ranks that exercises an ungodly influence over a geographical area (that is, city, region, county, state, nation).

Prophecy – This is an ability to prophesy, by the unction of the Holy Spirit, some past, present, or future event which brings encouragement, comfort, and edification to the Body of Christ.

Prophet – One who speaks forth the mind of God about a current or future event.

Prophetic –One who has spiritual gifts that are of a revelatory nature.

Prophetic Act – Physical acts of faith or declaration, done in the natural, to reflect and agree with a prophetic sense of what God is about to do.

Prophetic Atmosphere – Is described as a strong presence of the Lord, prompting, and unction of the Holy Spirit for prophetic ministry.

Prophetic Expressions – Prophetic expressions (that is, dreams, visions, impressions, song of the Lord) are manifestations flowing from the four revelation gifts: word of knowledge, word of wisdom, discernment of spirits, and prophecy.

Prophetic Intercession – See Chapter 2

Prophetic Intercessor – Someone who is called a prophetic intercessor usually has at least *one* of the following four revelation gifts (word of knowledge, the word of wisdom, the discernment of spirits, and prophecy) operating in their intercessory expression.

Prophetic Promises – Prophetic words spoken under the unction of the Holy Spirit; verses found in scripture that are biblical promises of God's truth.

Prophetic Seasons – A particular time frame in which God has determined certain events to happen.

Prophetic Sensing – Spiritual discernment or an impression that may come in the form of a vague perception of something that God is revealing.

Prophetic Thread – Identifying the over-arching theme of what God is speaking. In the context of a prayer meeting there may be a lot God has revealed through the prophetic gifts in operation. The prophetic thread is the main idea or pattern of what God is communicating.

R

Rahab Spirit – A demonic spirit characterized by chaos and confusion (Isaiah 51:9; Job 26:12).

Rebuking – In the context of dealing with an evil spirit, it is an exercise of a believer's spiritual authority over a demonic spirit. Usually a rebuke is a command for a evil spirit to leave.

Redemption – To the believer, this term is an expression of the price Jesus paid with His blood in securing our salvation.

Redemptive Gift – In reference to the spiritual gifts outlined in Romans 12. All spiritual gifts are given by God to further equip believers in fulfilling the great commission.

Redemptive Purpose – A phrase to reference God's purpose and special grace upon a land or a people group within a geographical area that can cause the further release of God's plan of salvation message to spread.

Revelation – Knowledge and wisdom revealing the mind and the will of God.

Revelation Gifts – There are four spiritual gifts identified in I Corinthians 12: 7-10: word of knowledge, word of wisdom, discernment of spirits and prophecy that are revelatory in the expression of those gifts.

Revelation Knowledge – Knowledge revealed by God.

Revival – a move of God where many people come to a saving knowledge of Christ Jesus.

Rhema Word – When God speaks through his written Word as a current Word of revelation to that individual.

Rulers of Darkness – Demonic spirits who oversee geographical areas and regions.

S

Schemes – A plot or a plan used by the devil to trick or deceive people.

Scribe – A person who takes handwritten notes to later reference.

Seductive spirit – A demonic spirit that tempts people to view a sinful action as attractive or appealing.

Seer – A person with a prophetic gift that enables them to see into the spirit realm.

Shepherds – A biblical symbol of pastors. A spiritual gift to the body of Christ for the purpose of oversight and care in the equipping of believers for the work of the ministry.

Soulish – Something that is characterized as coming from the soul realm (the mind, will, or emotions).

Soul Realm – The place where our mind, will, and emotions exercises its influence concerning our thoughts, beliefs, and behavior.

Sphere of Influence – The circle of people with whom you come into regular contact (family, friends, workplace, etc) where you have an ability to influence others.

Spirit-filled Church – A term referring to a church who embraces the gifts and manifestations of the Holy Spirit.

Spiritual Activity – The movement of demonic or angelic activity within a particular location or area.

Spiritual Atmosphere or Climate – A reference to discerning the spiritual environment as to whether there is a demonic, angelic, or divine activity in a particular area or location.

Spiritual Attack – A specific demonic attack or plan to oppose believers.

Spiritual Battle – Demonic forces in opposition to believers.

Spiritual Breakthrough – The ability to move forward in fulfilling the great commission.

Spiritual Gifts – When one becomes a Christian, there are gift(s) given to empower the believer in fulfilling the great commission (1 Corinthians 12)

Spiritual Mapping – Spiritual mapping is the process of discerning what may be blocking the gospel from having a greater impact in a geographical area. There are two essential elements to the success of this kind of a team: gifted researchers and prophetic intercessors. The focus for a mapping team is to identify spiritual strongholds that have been established through an historical event, declaration, or cultural tradition.

Spiritual Realm – Another dimension of reality where spiritual beings, angels and demons are clearly seen in the context of the spiritual conflict that is part of our earthly existence.

Spiritual Warfare – Demonic opposition that opposes the advancement of the church in fulfilling the great commission.

Stewardship – The faithful management of something entrusted into our care.

Strategems – Methods that are carefully planned by the enemy to tempt us into sin. These methods are hidden like ambushes in the circumstances we face and include sudden or impulsive thoughts to do wrong, hindrances or obstacles, discouragement, fears, lies or deception, sickness, word curses activated through murmuring, complaining, gossip, or slander spoken yourself or spoken by another person about you.

Strategic Level Intercession – Spiritual warfare having to do with a higher demonic rank such as a principality in operation over a specific geographical area.

Stronghold – A system of demonically inspired lies that people believe as truth.

Synergy – A Holy Spirit enabling that increases the effectiveness of a ministry with the collaboration of certain parts of the body of Christ or spiritual gifts working together.

T

The Great Commission – The command for all believers to go out into all the world and share the message of salvation (Matthew 28:19-20).

Transformation – The process of individual people or a people group in a particular geographical area experiencing a spiritual encounter with God that changes their belief system of truth by entering into a redemptive relationship to Him. This encounter is so profound that the resulting change in ones behavior begins to impact all levels of society within their sphere of influence in addition to the land itself.

U

Unction of the Holy Spirit – A spiritual prompting of God.

V

Vindication – For truth to be revealed resulting with one being set free from allegation or blame.

Visions – Picture or a series of pictures we see in our mind that reveal a message from the Lord.

W

Warfare – Demonic opposition to oppose believers from fulfilling their divine calling or destiny as it relates to the spreading the gospel message.

Warfare Prayer – Prayer that confronts demonic opposition that is impacting individual believers, the body of Christ, a city, or a nation by utilizing our spiritual authority in Christ, the word of God (logos) and our spiritual weapons.

War-Zone – A battleground; an expression to describe the spiritual condition of our earthly existence.

Watchman – One called to watch and pray with an assignment that may be the result of the declaration of a prophetic word that has yet to be fulfilled over a geographical area or the fulfillment of a local church vision God has revealed to the leadership (Isaiah 62:6-7; Jeremiah 1:11-12).

Witchcraft – Accessing secret knowledge or power other than through the Holy Spirit is a violation of scripture. Therefore, consulting with angels, demons or spirit guides, participating in séances, reading tarot cards, palm reading, seeking the counsel of a medium, and casting spells are all a counterfeit means of accessing spiritual knowledge and power.

Word Curse – Words spoken to call down harm or evil on someone's life or circumstances. Words spoken with an evil intent can carry a demonic power that can become a harassing form of spiritual opposition.

Word of Knowledge – It is the sudden knowledge of a past, present, or future fact about a particular person or situation without any prior knowledge. When this gift is working, it is clear that only the Lord could have revealed the fact or understanding.

Word of Wisdom – It is a sudden knowing of God's wisdom in a situation for either how to pray for the prayer need or what actions to take. I think of this gift as *knowledge applied*. The key characteristic to a word of wisdom is having a clear sense of direction.

Worldly Influence – Attitudes and actions that reflect our carnal nature, with its lusts and desires, which are at odds with the spirit of God.

Suggested Reading

Below are some of my most favorite authors and book titles that have impacted my life. I have listed these as a resource and encourage you to check into other books these authors have written.

Apostles and the Emerging Apostolic Movement by David Cannistraci
  ISBN 0830723382
  www.DavidCannistraci.org

Beyond the Veil by Alice Smith
  ISBN 0830720707
  www.eddieandalice.com

Confronting the Powers by C.Peter Wagner
  ISBN 0-83007-1819-2

Dreams and Visions by Jane Hamon
  ISBN 0-939868-19-9
  www.ciresourcecenter.com

God's Vision for Your Church by David Cannistraci
  ISBN 0-8307-2515
  www.DavidCannistraci.org

Prayer-walking: Praying On Site with Insight by Steve Hawthorne and Graham Kendrick
  ISBN 0-88419-268-7

Prophetic Intercession by Barbara Wentroble
  ISBN 0-8307-2376-5
  ISBN 0-8307-3279-9
  www.internationalbreakthroughministries.org

Possessing the Gates by Cindy Jacobs
  ISBN 0-8007-9187-9
  www.generals.org

Releasing the Prophetic Destiny of a Nation by Dutch
Sheets and Chuck Pierce
 ISBN 0768422841
 www.dutchsheets.org
 www.glory-of-zion.org

That None Should Perish by Ed Silvoso
 ISBN 0-8307-1688-2
 www.harvestevangelism.org

The Power of One Christ-Like Life by Francis Frangipane
 ISBN 0-88368-628-7
 www.frangipane.org

The Seer by Jim W. Goll
 ISBN 0-7684-2232-9
 www.jimgoll.com

The Spiritual Man by Watchman Nee
 ISBN 9780935008395

The Three Battlegrounds by Francis Frangipane
 ISBN 0-9629049-0-2
 www.frangipane.org

Transforming Grace: God's Path to Life and Inward Change by Jim Johnson
 ISBN-10-9815905-3-5
 www.JimJohnsonMissions.com

What to Wear to War by Warren W. Wiersbe
 ISBN 0-8474-6515-2

Made in the USA
Charleston, SC
06 March 2010